Madden v. Lifecord, Inc.

A biotechnology case in product liability, conversion, medical malpractice, negligence, wrongful death, breach of contract, breach of the duty of good faith and misrepresentation

Victoria Sutton, M.P.A., Ph.D., J.D.
Professor of Law
Texas Tech University School of Law

IN THE UNITED STATES DISTRICT COURT
FOR THE NORTHERN DISTRICT OF NEW COLUMBIA

John Madden, et. al. Plaintiff	)))	
v.	))	No. 01-27255
Lifecord,Inc. et. al. Defendant	))))	

VARGAS PUBLISHING
Copyright © 2018 by Victoria Sutton

This book is typeset in Times New Roman Style. The paper used in this book meets the specifications for 60# white 444ppi.

ISBN-13: 978-0-9968186-3-6 (paperback)
Printed and Manufactured in the United States of America
First printing, 2004 by the National Trial Advocacy Institute
Second printing, 2018 by Vargas publishing
Typeset in the U.S.A.

Published and distributed in North America by
Vargas Publishing
P.O. Box 6801
Lubbock, TX 79461
http://www.vargaspublishing.com

Acknowledgments

This trial practice exercise has been developed with the assistance of the students who enrolled in my Law and Biotechnology and Law and Science courses.

For comments and criticisms, I thank Professors Timothy Floyd, Daniel Benson, Robert Weninger, Jorge Ramirez and Susan Fortney of Texas Tech University School of Law, who participated in the shaping of this case in their role as judge in numerous trail practice student exercises. Specifically, I also thank Professor Timothy Floyd, who has taught legal skills courses for many years, for his willingness to review these materials and his insightful comments. I also want to thank Professor Daniel Hardy, from the Department of Biochemistry and Dr. Ronald Kennedy, from the Department of Microbiology for their comments on the medical and scientific issues in the case. And thanks, also, to Dean Walter Huffman who supported the value of the work to develop this course and this publication.

I also owe much gratitude to Professor Anthony Morella who was the first to demonstrate to me that trial practice could be taught -- and learned, when I was enrolled in his trial practice class at American University, Washington College of Law.

Also, I wish to acknowledge the following for allowing the use of their work for this publication:

Crump, David, "Basic Methods of Qualifying or Introducing Some Common Items of Evidence," Texas Bar Journal 702-3 (July 1980).

Danthinne, X. (2001) Simultaneous Insertion of Two expression cassettes into Adenovirus Vectors. BioTechniques 30(3):612-6, 618-9.
For the AdenoQuick adenovirus process graphic.

Garland publishing, Taylor & Francis Group, for use of the lifecycle of retrovirus graphic from *Essential Cell Biology* (1998).

Kimball, Dr. John W., for the use of the retroviruses graphic.

Obiogene, Inc. for the use of the adenoviruses graphic.

Wired News, Dec. 20, 2001 article: Cord Blood Banks/Critics Decry commercialism.

Madden v. Lifecord, Inc.

TABLE OF CONTENTS

I. INTRODUCTION

This case file and materials present a fact pattern with many of the types of materials that would be part of a trial involving issues in biotechnology. This exercise focuses on the use of expert witnesses. As with any trial preparation, a thorough reading of the entire case file and an understanding of the exhibits is important. The materials in this file are those kinds of exhibits and evidence that would be developed during pre-trial discovery, such as depositions and production of documents. You may also want to practice assembling a trial notebook with this exercise.

This trial practice exercise is used ideally in a courtroom setting, with individuals playing the role of expert witnesses, one or more judges and the rest of the members of the class serving as jurors. Wearing proper attire for the day of your presentation is expected.

This case file also includes basic trial practice guidance for the important elements of the trial that should assist you in preparation. Advocacy is an art and a skill and there is no better way to learn than to practice in a trial practice setting.

The synopsis of this case file is as follows:

Jerry and Sally Madden are a couple in Bellville, New Columbia who were expecting their first child, contracted to preserve and store their baby's umbilical cord stem cells for use in the event of manifestation of a number of diseases that could be treated with stem cells, and signed an agreement with Lifecord, Inc. in Hopesville, California. Jerry Madden, the Plaintiff alleges that he made payments as agreed in the written contract between Plaintiff and Defendant, but the check was apparently lost in the mail. The Defendant, Lifecord, claims the Maddens defaulted on their contract. In an equipment failure of the cooling system maintained by Lifecord, Inc., many of the stem cells were destroyed, including those of the Madden's child. The Maddens allege that the defendant was negligent in failing to have a backup cooling system. The plaintiff also alleges that the method of creating the stem cell product for treatment was defective, and did not met the current scientific standard for such treatments. By the time that Plaintiff requested the stem cells from Lifecord, Inc. for treatment of a diagnosed leukemia in their son, they discovered that the defendant, thinking the Maddens were in default on the enrollment agreement, had sold half of the stem cells to an estranged aunt who needed them for treatment of her own leukemia. The few stem cells that remained were fewer than needed for treatment of the Maddens's child.

When the Maddens discovered that Lifecord, Inc. had not received their payment, they paid the defendant the last enrollment payment, then received the remaining stem cells which were used in treatment of the Madden's child. The defendant used an adenovirus mediated transfer of interferon to the umbilical cord blood stem cells in order to treat the leukemia. While this process has been published in the scientific literature, later publications recommend the use of the retrovirus, rather than the adenovirus. (The adenovirus dies too quickly and before not enough of the interferon genes can be transferred to the stem cells by the adenovirus).

Lifecord, Inc. utilized the very small number of stem cells that they knew were insufficient to treat the leukemia in the Plaintiff. Lifecord, Inc. was also aware that the quantity of stem cells was directly proportional to the success of the treatment.

The Madden's child did not recover from the leukemia and died within two months of the treatment, on October 15, 2011.

You are representing one of the parties in the lawsuit filed by the Maddens in the District Court of New Columbia. Each party has two expert witnesses, and ample depositions and exhibits for trial.

Best of luck.

II. APPROACH TO TRIAL PRACTICE

Becoming familiar with the materials in the entire case file is an essential first step in this trial practice exercise. A group of students for the plaintiff will form one law firm; and a group of students to represent the defendant will form another law firm. A team of three students, with two expert witnesses and two opposing expert witnesses, for example, will have the opportunity to do two of the following assignments: a direct examination, a cross examination, an opening or closing statement.

Outside preparation of expert witnesses is required to prepare for their direct examination. The opposing party, of course, should not talk to the expert witness and will have only the benefit of the expert's deposition and any publications. The opposing party should not talk to the opposing expert witnesses outside of the courtroom.

Having a judge and jury is essential, and students who may not be at the table for trial, should participate as jurors.

Setting time limits for each part of the trial is important for the trial practice, and in real practice, time limits are typical.

Early on, you should establish the time limits for parts of the trial practice:

Opening statements: ____ minutes

Voir dire   ____ minutes

Direct examination: ____ minutes

Cross examination: ____ minutes

Closing statements: ____ minutes

The order of the trial will be as follows:

Opening statement ----plaintiff
Opening statement-----defendant

[Fact witnesses are optional, and if you do not use fact witnesses you still need their evidence and testimony, the court taking judicial notice that it is already in the record.]

Plaintiff fact witnesses:
Jerry Madden, father of Conrad Madden

Alex Henley, M.D.

Defendant fact witnesses:
Skyler Sorenson, M.D., Vice President for Research, Lifecord, Inc.
Dr. Sorenson will testify that the informed consent and all procedures were followed sufficiently and in accord with company policies. Sorenson will also testify that the Plaintiff failed to make

payments as agreed, resulting in releasing the Defendant from any contractual obligations.

Loren McCaffery, Ph.D., Director of the Lifecord Center, Lifecord, Inc.
Dr. McCaffery will testify to the receipt of payments, the written contract, the sale of the stem cells to Plaintiff=s estranged aunt, as well as the incident involving the failure of the liquid nitrogen tank backup system.

Voir dire of each expert witness.

Plaintiff's experts
        Dr. B. Jan Cummings, M.D.
                Voir dire, plaintiff's attorney
                Direct examination, plaintiff's attorney
                Cross examination, defendant's attorney
                Re-direct examination, plaintiff's attorney (optional)
                Re-cross examination, defendant's attorney (optional)

        Dr. Randal T. Kramer, Ph.D.
                Voir dire, plaintiff's attorney
                Direct examination, plaintiff's attorney
                Cross examination, defendant's attorney
                Re-direct examination, plaintiff's attorney (optional)
                Re-cross examination, defendant's attorney (optional)

        Motion for directed verdict, defendant's attorney

Defendant's expert witnesses
        Dr. Samuel Abramowitz, M.D.
                Voir dire, defendant's attorney
                Direct examination, defendant's attorney
                Cross examination, plaintiff's attorney
                Re-direct examination, defendant's attorney (optional)
                Re-cross examination, plaintiff's attorney (optional)

        Dr. Samuel J. Meselson, M.D.
                Voir dire, defendant's attorney
                Direct examination, defendant's attorney
                Cross examination, plaintiff's attorney
                Re-direct examination, defendant's attorney (optional)
                Re-cross examination, plaintiff's attorney (optional)

        Motion for directed verdict, plaintiff's attorney

Closing argument, plaintiff's attorney
Closing argument, defendant's attorney

III.   Witness Preparation

It is essential that the litigation teams spend some outside class time with their expert witnesses to prepare them for direct examination as well as anticipated questions on cross examination. A faculty member, or graduate student from a relevant discipline or a non-law student is best for role-playing the expert witness; however, another law student from the class could benefit from the experience playing the expert witness. In order to prepare the expert witness, it is essential that the person playing the expert become familiar with the expert's resume, and the types of evidence that they will be expected to explain. It becomes painfully obvious when a student has failed to prepare their expert witness for the trial practice exercise, and may be a hard-learned lesson.

When the attorney meets with their expert witness, they should come prepared with questions for *voir dire* and direct examination and should go over those questions with the expert witness. A good trial attorney should never ask a question that he/she does not know what will be the answer. Only with substantial experience (or in a movie script) should an attorney venture into the unknown with a line of questioning. The purpose of this rehearsal is not to tell the expert what to say, but rather to make sure that the question elicits the type of evidence which the trial attorney needs to establish every element of the case, including the qualifications of the expert witness. Failure to make the relevant expert testimony a part of the record may result in a grant of a motion for a directed verdict at the end of the evidence.

In preparation for cross-examination, the attorney should review the anticipated questions which will arise for the expert witness based upon problem statements in the deposition or problems with flaws in the scientific evidence and exhibits. This, too, is important because after the cross-examination, there will be no time to explain rehabilitation or to explain to the expert what must be clarified for the record, when the attorney has only one chance for re-direct examination.

You should give your expert witness some quick tips on testifying. As a general matter, you may want to suggest to the expert they should think of his/her role as teaching the judge or jury the information that is important in a clear and understandable way. You may also want to suggest to your expert they avoid changing disposition or demeanor when they are answering questions for either the plaintiff's attorney or the defendant's attorney. Looking hostile or combative with the opposing counsel almost never works in your favor. Suggest to the expert that they be prepared to speak without excessively reading. This could take some additional preparation and practice before the trial. Looking relaxed, confident and believable is the goal for your expert. Finally, remind your expert that they should not speak with opposing counsel, unless in a deposition, with you, present.

IV.   Pre-Trial Motions

The pre-trial motions include the motion *in limine* and the motion for summary judgment.

The motion *in limine*, is literally the motions before the trial begins. They can include the objection to the testimony being offered or objection to the qualifications of the expert for the type of testimony that the expert expects to proffer. The motion can address any or all of the experts' qualifications and their testimony.

The motion for summary judgement, if granted, requires that the court dismiss the case with prejudice against the party which has failed to carry their burden of showing that evidence will be introduced to prove every element of their case. One way to succeed on a motion for summary judgment is to eliminate an element of their claim, by eliminating the testimony to establish that element. In this case, the focus is on the testimony of the expert witness. Failure to have any expert survive a motion *in limine* may result in the elimination of the testimony which would support one of the essential elements of the case--- in this case, a toxic tort. Without testimony and an expert opinion to establish one of the elements of a tort, then a motion for summary judgment would be appropriate to dismiss that claim.

V.   *Voir Dire*

The *voir dire* is an interview with the expert witness, including name, academic and professional credentials as well as relevant experience. The *voir dire* is conducted by the plaintiff's expert witnesses and by the defendant of the defendant's expert witnesses. This process typically begins with the attorney asking the expert witness a series of questions about their background, for example, "What was your undergraduate major?", "In what subject do you hold a graduate degree?" "Is that a Ph.D. or doctoral degree?" Of course, the attorney will know all the answers to these questions, but it is necessary to lay the foundation for the qualifications of the expert witness so that they may be admitted as an expert witness and testify as an expert and render opinions.

This process serves another purpose, as well as putting qualifications on the record. The *voir dire* provides the first opportunity for the expert witness to meet the judge and jury and this is the time to make positive first impressions on both. The attorney should draw out questions which will allow the expert to make eye-contact with the jury and to allow the jury to gain trust and confidence in the expert witness. The *voir dire* also serves the purpose of providing a warm-up for the attorney to have an exchange with the expert witness, developing a rapport for the judge and jury before the critical questions are necessarily presented for the expert witness's response.

In this trial practice exercise, resumes are provided in the exhibits section for use for the roles of each of the experts. If it is decided that resumes can be revised, copies of the revised resume must be brought to the courtroom on the day of the trial and presented to the opposing attorneys before trial, and before questioning at the latest point.

VI. Direct, Cross, Redirect and Recross Examination

Direct examination

Direct examination of an expert witness gives the attorney the opportunity to elicit the required testimony and opinions from their own expert witness for the record. Prior preparation is essential and the practice of reviewing the questions with the expert will help ensure that the trial strategy will be effective. Questioning may not be leading, and the testimony must come from the expert witness, not from the attorney.

Cross examination

Cross examination is the opportunity for the opposing attorney to examine the expert witness on weaknesses in the testimony in an effort to discredit the expert=s credibility or to discredit the expert conclusions. Questions may be leading, and should be leading, eliciting a Ayes@ or Ano@ response, only, when possible. Keeping control of the questioning is an important strategy on cross-examination.

Redirect examination

Redirect examination is not required, but if the expert witness has been impeached, this allows an opportunity for the attorney to rehabilitate the witness. Here, the questions must not be leading, and may be risky if the expert witness is not prepared for this contingency.

Recross examination

Recross examination is rarely done, and may not be permitted. Recross may be allowed for one or two questions if necessary to clarify the testimony of the expert witness.

VII.   Impeachment and Rehabilitation

Impeachment of any expert witness will require the opposing attorney to rehabilitate the expert witness, if the attorney decides this is possible at the close of cross-examination. It is during re-direct examination that the attorney has the opportunity to repair any damage done to the testimony or credibility of the expert witness during the cross-examination.

In impeachment by prior inconsistent statement, the opposing attorney may confront the witness during cross examination if the issue was raised in the direct examination. If the witness denies making the inconsistent statement, then the document or evidence may be introduced for purposes of impeachment. Federal Rule of Evidence 613(b) provides that the witness must be "afforded an opportunity to explain or deny" the prior inconsistent statement in order to allow the admission of evidence that will be used to impeach this witness.

In this case, Brandon Chapel, M.D., is the most likely expert witness who will need rehabilitation based upon some of the testimony given in his deposition. However, any witness may be damaged during cross-examination and require clarification of testimony, which is a form of rehabilitation.

If rehabilitation fails, then the impeachment of the testimony of that expert witness may prove devastating to the case.

VIII.   Introduction of Exhibits

The introduction of exhibits is another skill that is important to any trial. The introduction of exhibits requires that the attorney lay a foundation for the introduction of the evidence by identifying the evidence and why the expert witness knows what it is. This establishes that the document is what it purports to be, for example, the reports and depositions of the expert witnesses.

The attorney introducing the exhibits must remember that in laying the foundation, he/she must establish that the testimony is both authentic and relevant and that it complies with hearsay rules and the best evidence rules. Authenticity is simply that the document or evidence is what it purports to be. Relevance means that the evidence must link with an issue being proven. It does not have to prove the entire issue, but may be only a brick in the wall of proving an issue.

The document must be submitted to the court (a clerk or the judge) and marked and numbered as an exhibit. The attorney may number the documents before the hearing, but this does not allow for documents that may be excluded, or changes in strategy or order. Thereafter, that testimony should be referred to by exhibit number, so each attorney should keep a list of the exhibits and the numbers assigned by the court.

The attorney should then ask the witness to identify the document. The attorney may hand the document to the witness for examination. When the witness has responded, the attorney may then ask something about the nature of the evidence, for example, is this document the deposition you gave on May 3, 2011?

An exercise involving only the expert witnesses, noted below, can be done with this casefile. The following list of exhibits should be used by the attorneys and introduced through the expert witnesses:

1.   Resume of Samuel Abramowitz, M.D.
2,   Deposition of Samuel Abramowitz, M.D.
3.   Abramowitz deposition, Attachment 15, New York Times article
4.   Abramowitz deposition, Attachment 1, Adenoviruses
5.   Abramowitz deposition, Attachment 2, Life Cycle of a Retrovirus
6.   Abramowitz deposition, Attachment 3, MedicalLine Abstract 1997
7.   Abramowitz deposition, Attachment 4, MedicalLine Abstract 1999
8.   Resume of Randal T. Kramer, Ph.D.
9.   Deposition of Randal T. Kramer, Ph.D.
10.   Kramer Deposition, Attachment A, Lifecord Storage facilities
11.   Resume of Samuel Meselson
12.   Deposition of Samuel Meselson
13.   Meselson deposition, Attachment P, Lifecord photos of Madden cord blood
14.   Meselson deposition, Attachment Q, Lifecord webpage, forms
15.   Meselson deposition, Attachment L, article Wired News, Cord Blood Banks
16.   Resume of Jan Cummings, Ph.D.
17.   Deposition of Cummings
18.   Cummings deposition, Attachment 5, Rate of survival of CD34+cells, webpage
19.   Cummings deposition, Attachment 6, Abstract

The following list of exhibits are to be introduced through the fact witnesses:

For Loren McCaffery:
1.   Payment record for Lifecord, showing payments of Maddens on Nov 20 $100 with birth, Nov 29 $1000 and Jan 15, Feb 15, Mar 15, Apr 15, and May 15.
2.   Telephone log

For Jerry Madden:
1.   Copies of cancelled checks from Maddens for these payment due dates:
   Nov. 20 #849
   Nov. 29 #853
   Dec. 15 #864
   Jan. 15 #885
   Feb. 15 #899
   Mar. 15 #919
   Apr. 15 # 936
   May 15 #955
   June 15 #1122

How to Introduce Exhibits

1. Introducing a Photograph into Evidence

Step 1:   Have the exhibit marked by the court reporter.
Step 2:   Have the witness identify it and lay the predicate for its admissibility. (NOTE: it is unethical to expose inflammatory exhibits to jury view before they are admitted. Some trial lawyers do so routinely, for a simple reason: they are unethical)
Q: Mr. Plaintiff, I show you what has been marked plaintiff's exhibit no. 1, and I ask you whether you can identify it. Can you?
A: Yes, I can.
Q: What is it?
A: It's a photograph showing the damage to my care after the accident I've just told about.
Q: And does it truly and accurately reflect what the car looked like at that time?
A: Yes, it does.

Step 3:   You have now laid the predicate for introduction of the exhibit. You should now walk over to opposing counsel and tender it to him/her.

Step 4:   Formally offer the exhibit into evidence. "Your honor, at this time I offer plaintiff's exhibit no. 1 into evidence.

Step 5:   Youropponent may now object. You should be ready to make a short argument in support of your exhibit. "Your Honor, even though the cost of repairs have been stipulated as my opponent says, the exhibit is still relevant to the way in which the accident happened." You should make this argument only if it seems appropriate, that is, you should remain quiet if the judge overrules the objection away.

Step 6:   If an objection is sustained and you think the evidence is both admissible and important, ask further questions directed to laying the predicate for it.

Step 7:   Be sure the exhibit is formally received by the judge.

Step 8:   If it seems desireable, ask to have the exhibit passed by the bailiff to the jury or ask the witness to read excerpts from it if it is a document.

2.   Introducing a Tangible Object
    (Note: the steps outlined above for marking the exhibit, offering it, etc. apply generally to objects and documents. They will not be repeated here but should be done. The predicate is as follows:)
    Q: I show you what has been marked as plaintiff's exhibit 2 and ask you whether you can identify it. Can you?
    A: Yes.
    Q: What is it?
    A: It is the actual steering wheel of the car I was driving at the time.

Q: How do you recognize it?

A: [Here there can be a variety of answers. "Because I drove that car for 3 years and I know its appearance." "Because it contains a crack at the top where I hit my head in this accident." "Because my initials and the date of the accident are scratched on the side of it, here, and I put them there when it was removed from the car."

A word to the wise: Tangible objects whether they be guns, bent fenders, leg casts, fingerprints, etc., often have an evidentiary value greater than their relevance to the issues in the case; and even if you have had the cracked steering wheel described thoroughly by testimony it will probably enhance your case to introduce it.

3.   Introducing a Business Record

Business records are hearsay. They constitute out-of-court statements offered to prove the matter stated in them. However, there is an exception to the hearsay rule for business records meeting certain qualifications. The questions and answers that would qualify them might be as follows (after the witness' name and background has been given):

Q: Do you have actual care, custody and control of the business records of Joe's Auto Shop?

A: Yes. [A qualified witness other than the custodian may sometimes be proper, but to be sure, get the custodian.]

Q: Are these records kept and prepared by Joe's Auto Repair in the ordinary course of business?

A: Yes.

Q: Are the entries made at or about the time of the events they record?

A: Yes.

Q: Are they made initiatlly by someone who has personal knowledge of the events recorded?

A: Yes. [Again, personal knowledge of the entrant is not always required, but a "yes" answer here makes introduction easier.]

Note: It is a good idea to go over these questions carefully with the witness to ensure that he/she understands them. An auto repairman may get thrown by a mumbo-jumbo phrase such as "at or about the time of the events they record," even though it is required by the business records stattue, and may answer erroneously with the result that introduction fo the records becomes difficult.

Second Note: Once the records are received in evidence you can have the witness "interpret" them. For example, if one of the issues in the case concerned the plaintiff's brakes:

Q: What work , if any, do these records show was done approximately 8 weeks before this occurrence on March 21, 1977?

A: A complete brake job. Here where it says "linings," that's brake linings, and this line here lists the other parts. And there's labor.

Q: Does the record reflect whether the automobile was road tested?

A: It was.

4. Qualification of an Expert Witness

The expert may be anything from a garage mechanic to a metallurgist. He may be qualified by experience along, by training along, or by both. Question sand answers to do so might go something like this (after the witness' name and background have been elicited:)

Q: What is your occupation or profession?

A: I'm a metallurgist. That means I study and work with metals. [Or: I'm a mechanic at Joe's Auto Shop.]

Q: What qualifications do you have for the work --- what education, training or experience?

A: I have an AB in physics from Harvard and a PhD in metallurgy from the California Institute of Technology. I am on the faculty of the University of Texas, department of physics, where I teach metallurgical courses; I am a member of the American Society of Metallurgists. I worked 10 years in industry and am the author of 25 articles in learned journals.. [Or: I done worked as a mechanic for nigh onto 30 year. I was borned into this line of work and I done fixed thousands of folks' cars. I know just about all there is to know about how to fix brake systems on cars like this one here. It's how I make my livin'.]

Introduce resume of the expert as an exhibit, and then ask the expert to identify it.

Q: Is this a copy of your resume?

A: Yes, it is.

Q: I ask the court to accept Dr. _____ as an expert in the field of metallurgy.

Note: At this point, the opposing counsel has an opportunity to object, but this is rarely done. Only if the field for which the expert is qualifying is not appropriate or is so unusual that the opposing counsel may want to object.

Once the expert has been qualified, he may be asked (1) a hypothetical question base don facts in evidence in the case, (2) a question based on his own examination of objects involved, or (3) a combination of both.

Q: All right, now, Mr. Mechanic, you say you saw Plaintiff's car after the brakes were fixed. In your opinion, were they fixed properly, so that they'd stop the care normally?

A: Yes, they were.

Q: Then, let me ask you the following question, based on the facts and testimony in this case. If plaintiff were driving 30 mph on a dry asphalt road and applied the brakes suddenly, would the car continue to respond to steering as it stopped?

A: You could still steer it, just like if you wasn't applying no brakes at all.

Q: Then I take it that the car, in you opinion, would not veer sharply into the other land (as one witness has said) if it was steered straight ahead?

A: No. It wouldn't.

Adapted from: David Crump, *Basic Methods of Qualifying or Introducing Some Common Items of Evidence*, Texas Bar Journal, July 1980.

IX.   Pleadings File

IN THE UNITED STATES DISTRICT COURT
FOR THE NORTHERN DISTRICT OF NEW COLUMBIA

John Madden, et. al.   ·)
  Plaintiff   )
)
   v.   )   No. 01-27255
)
Lifecord,Inc. et. al.   )
  Defendant   )
)
_____)

COMPLAINT

FOR WRONGFUL DEATH, NEGLIGENCE, MISREPRESENTATION
PRODUCT LIABILITY, CONVERSION, BREACH OF CONTRACT

Jurisdiction and Parties

Jurisdiction in this case is based upon diversity of citizenship and the amount in controversy. Plaintiff, Madden is a citizen of the State of New Columbia. Defendant, Lifecord, Inc. is a corporation incorporated under the laws of the State of California, having its principal place of business in a state other than the State of New Columbia. The amount in controversy exceeds, exclusive of interest and costs, the sum of seventy-five thousand ($75,000) dollars.

Statement of the Case

Jerry and Sally Madden were expecting their first child, when the Hillhouse Hospital staff physician approached them about the possibility of preserving their baby's umbilical cord stem cells for use in the event of manifestation of a number of diseases which could be treated with stem cells.

Defendant advertised on the internet its services to collect and store umbilical cord blood stem cells in a controlled, refrigerated storage unit kept at a constant -196 degrees Fahrenheit for up to five years, for the benefit of its donors. The Defendant charged Plaintiff for the service an enrollment fee, and yearly maintenance fees.

Plaintiff made payments as agreed in the written contract between Plaintiff and Defendant. The agreement was signed on November 20, 2011, and the $100.00, nonrefundable deposit was paid to the Defendant, the day that their child, Conrad Madden was born. A payment of $1,000.00 was made on November 29, 2011 in accordance with Defendant's enrollment agreement. The first of seven enrollment payments were due on December 15, 2011, and on the 15th of each month, thereafter. Defendant received payments for January 15th, February 15th, March 15th, April 15th and May 15th, in the amount of $200, each.

The final enrollment payment for June 15th was not received by the Defendant because it was lost in the mail. The annual payment was not due until November 15th, 2011. Plaintiff did not have notice of this until Plaintiff requested the stem cells from Defendant on September 7, 2011. At that time, Plaintiff also discovered that Defendant had sold half of the Plaintiff's stem cells to Plaintiff's estranged aunt, Ms. Sarah Whitting, on June 19, 2011, for her own illness.

Plaintiff learned that half of the remaining cells had been lost when the storage unit failed and the temperature dropped to a level which resulted in the death of half of the remaining stem cells on August 30, 2011. This, the Plaintiff learned, was the result of the Defendant having discontinued the use of the backup system which ensured that if the liquid nitrogen tanks emptied, that the backup system would take over the cooling function. When the tanks ran out of liquid nitrogen one weekend, the backup cooling system was not available and the primary coolant system failed to maintain the required temperature.

The Plaintiff paid the Defendant the last enrollment payment on September 7, 2011 immediately upon discovering that Defendant had not received the payment and proceeded with the withdrawal of the stem cells, in order to treat leukemia in the Plaintiff, which had been diagnosed August 30, 2011.

Defendant used an adenovirus mediated transfer of interferon to the umbilical cord blood stem cells in order to treat the leukemia. While this process has been published in the scientific literature, later publications recommend the use of the retrovirus, rather than the adenovirus. The adenovirus dies too quickly and before enough of the interferon genes can be tranferred to the stem cells by the adenovirus.

Defendant further utilized the very small number of stem cells which the Defendant knew were insufficient to treat the leukemia in the Plaintiff. Defendant was aware that the quantity of stem cells was directly proportional to the success of the treatment.

As a result of Defendant's misrepresentation, negligence and faulty product design, the Plaintiff did not recover from the leukemia and died within two months of the treatment, on October 15, 2011.

Causes of Action

Count 1. Misrepresentation

1.   Defendant misrepresented the safety of the facilities,
stating that a backup cooling system was in place to prevent
accidentally allowing the stem cells to lose their frozen state.
     The failure of the primary cooling system without a backup
cooling system resulted in the loss of Plaintiff's stem cells.
Plaintiff relied upon Defendant's statements to his detriment.

Count 2. Conversion

2.   Defendant further caused the plaintiff's stem cells to be
intentionally taken from the storage facility without the
plaintiff or the plaintiff's guardian giving consent, resulting
in conversion of Plaintiff's property.

Count 3. Product Liability

3.   Defendant used a defective design when an alternative was
available for the engineered stem cell to be administered to the
Plaintiff, which caused serious injury and death to the
Plaintiff.

Count 4. Medical Malpractice

4.   Defendant proceeded with the engineering of the stem cells
without obtaining informed consent for the procedure from the
Plaintiff's guardian. Had Plaintiff's guardian understood the
procedure and the risks, Plaintiff would not have undergone the
procedure, resulting in statutory medical malpractice.

5.   Defendant owed a duty to reasonable care to the Plaintiff in
the procedure selected to prepare the stem cells for Plaintiff's
treatment. Defendant knowingly used a adenovirus transfer rather
than a retrovirus transfer, in the Plaintiff's treatment, while
the use of the retrovirus transfer was the standard of care for
stem cell treatments.

Count 5. Negligence

6.   Defendant owed a duty of ordinary care to Plaintiff to store
and protect the stem cells for Plaintiff's use in the event
Plaintiff developed one of the diseases which can be treated
with stem cells. Defendant breached that duty when the stem

cells were sold to Plaintiff's aunt. Due to the Defendant's negligence, the Defendant did not have either the quantity or the quality of stem cells to treat Plaintiff's leukemia.

7. Defendant owed a duty or ordinary care to Plaintiff to store and protect the stem cells for Plaintiff's use in the event Plaintiff developed one of the diseases which can be treated with stem cells.   These stem cells administered by the Defendant, failed to cure Plaintiff's leukemia because the Defendant did not have the quantity or the quality of the stem cells to administer a quantity that would successfully grow, due to the Defendant's negligence.

8. Plaintiff was in no way contributorily negligent.

Count 6. Wrongful Death

9. Defendant owed Plaintiff the duty of ordinary care. By failing to exercise reasonable care, Defendant breached the duty of ordinary care when Defendant allowed the storage unit to fail without a proper backup unit, destroying half of the stem cells, contributing to the lack of enough stem cells to successfully treat Plaintiff's leukemia and was the proximate cause of the Plaintiff's death.

Count 7. Breach of Contract

10. Defendant has breached the contract with Plaintiff, by selling Plaintiff's stem cells to Plaintiff's estranged aunt, contributing to the lack of enough stem cells to successfully treat Plaintiff's leukemia, resulting in damages to Plaintiff.

Count 8. Breach of the Duty of Good Faith

11. Defendant owed Plaintiff a duty of good faith and fair dealing with respect to Plaintiff's expectations of the advertised life-saving service provided by the Defendant. Defendant breached that duty of good faith when Defendant failed to contact the Plaintiff before selling the stem cells to Plaintiff's estranged aunt. Defendant's act was tortious in that Defendant knew or should have known that in the event that Plaintiff needed the stem cells they were no longer available. As a direct and proximate cause of this breach, Plaintiff died.

RELIEF REQUESTED

Wherefore, plaintiff prays that the court award the relief

as set forth below:
1. Compensatory and punitive damages of $5,000,000.
2. Lost wages in the amount of $200,000.
Submitted by:

Carole Cochran   11-20-2011
_____   _____
Carole Cochran, Esq.   Date
New Columbia Bar No. 698098
Attorney for the plaintiff

**IN THE UNITED STATES DISTRICT COURT
FOR THE NORTHERN DISTRICT OF NEW COLUMBIA**

John Madden, et. al.   )
    Plaintiffs   )
)
)
        v.   )   No. 01-27255
)
Lifecord, Inc. et. al.   )
    Defendant   )
)
_____)

ANSWER of Lifecord, Inc.

Defendant, Lifecord, does hereby deny all allegations made by the plaintiff, not herein expressly admitted, as permitted by Rule 8(b), Fed. R. Civ. P..

Defendant lacks knowledge or information sufficient to form a belief as to the truth of the allegations contained in plaintiff's Complaint, except as expressly set forth below.

Causes of Action

Count 1. Misrepresentation

Defendant denies ¶1 of Plaintiff's Original Complaint.

Count 2. Conversion
Defendant admits ¶2 of Plaintiff's Original Complaint, but denies last phrase of ¶2 that this was a conversion of Plaintiff's property.

Count 3. Product Liability

Defendant denies ¶3 in Plaintiff's Original Complaint. Defendant has failed to demonstrate a reasonable alternative design for the adenovirus mediated interferon transfer mechanism which produced the engineered stem cell which was administered to Plaintiff.

Count 4. Medical Malpractice

Defendant admits the first sentence of ¶4, but denies the

last sentence of ¶4 of Plaintiff's Original Complaint. Plaintiff is barred, in whole or in part, because Plaintiff knowingly agreed through informed consent given at the onset of the agreement, that the procedures could ultimately be performed for which the Plaintiff now complains.

Defendant denies ¶5 of Plaintiff's Original Complaint.

Defendant is not liable for any injuries resulting from Defendant's actions, because Plaintiff executed a release of liability at the time of the agreement between the parties.

Count 5. Negligence

Defendant denies ¶6 and ¶7 in Plaintiff's Original Complaint. Defendant is not negligent on the basis of the quantity of stem cells administered to Plaintiff, because the industry standard for quantity of stem cells administered was met. Defendant at all times exercised due care, and acted in accordance with reasonable and customary practice for the nation and for the community.

Count 6. Wrongful Death

Defendant denies ¶9 in the Plaintiff's Original Complaint. Defendant's actions were not the direct and proximate cause of the Plaintiff's death.

Count 7. Breach of Contract

Defendant performed the obligations in the contract with Plaintiff. When Plaintiff ceased making payments as agreed in the parties' written contract; Defendant commenced the sale of the Plaintiff's stem cells, which were agreed terms in the contract.

Count 8. Breach of the Duty of Good Faith

Defendant admits that Defendant advertises a life-saving service in ¶11 of the Plaintiff's Original Complaint. Defendant denies the remainder of ¶11.

Affirmative Defenses

Plaintiff was contributorily negligent in failing to ensure that enrollment payments had been received by the Defendant.

Defendant pleads the affirmative defense of failure of consideration.

Defendant pleads the affirmative defense of accord and satisfaction.

Defendant pleads that Plaintiff made material misrepresentations on the medical health history questionnaire.

Defendant pleads the affirmative defense of estoppel. Defendant is not liable for any injuries resulting from Defendant's actions, because Plaintiff executed a release of liability at the time of the agreement between the parties.

Defendant pleads the affirmative defense that the stem cell product through the adenovirus mediated transfer was neither unreasonably dangerous with respect to its manufacture and design nor was it defective. Intervening causes were the sole cause of Plaintiff's injuries.

Plaintiff's Complaint fails to state a cause of action upon which relief can be granted.

WHEREFORE, Defendant prays that Plaintiff take nothing against this Defendant and for such other relief to which this Defendant may justly show itself entitled.

Respectfully submitted:

_____*Jesse Doxin*_____   _____11-30-11_____

Jesse Doxin, Esq.   Date
New Columbia Bar 890123
Attorney for the defendant
Doxin, Doxin and Squiban, L.L.P.

IN THE UNITED STATES DISTRICT COURT
FOR THE NORTHERN DISTRICT OF NEW COLUMBIA

John Madden, et. al.   )
  Plaintiff   )
)
   v.   )   No. 01-27255
)
Lifecord, et. al.   )
  Defendant   )
)
_____)

DEFENDANT'S LIST
OF EXPERT WITNESSES

Pursuant to the Scheduling Order, dated September 25, 2011, Lifecord sets forth below its list of expert witnesses.

1. Arthur F. Pelman, M.D.

Position: George McPherson Professor of Medicine, Hardwood Medical School and Physician, Hillhouse Hospital, Consultant to Lifecord, Inc. and other blood banks.

Summary of Testimony: Dr. Pelman will testify that the stem cell procedures and Lifecord's process met the professional and industry standards.

2. Samuel Abramowitz, M.D.

Position: Professor of Medicine, New Columbia Medical School, Chair of the Immunology Department, Brigham & Bondary's Hospital.

Summary of Testimony: Dr. Abraham will testify that the process used by Defendant is essentially the same process he described in his published scientific papers in 1997.

3. Joseph D. Sanders, Ph.D.

    Position: Professor of Microbiology, University of New
Columbia, and County Health Officer in Bellville, New Columbia.

    Summary of Testimony: Dr. Sanders will testify that the
facilities were adequate for storing the frozen stem cells, and
facilities were as the company described them on their website.

4. Samuel J. Meselson, M.D.

    Position: Professor of Medicine, University of Bellville,
New Columbia.

    Summary of Testimony: Dr. Meselson will testify that he has
performed the stem cell treatment procedure and that the quantity
of the stem cells available for treatment has no relation with
the effectiveness.

5. John F. Hilton, Ph.D.

    Position: Associate Professor of Bioengineering, University
of New Columbia, Bellville, New Columbia.

    Summary of Testimony: Dr. Hilton will testify concerning the
stem cell procedure and the product design utilizing adenovirus
mediated transfer of interferon to the stem cells.

Respectfully submitted:

Jesse Doxin

Jesse Doxin, Esq.
New Columbia Bar 890123
Attorney for the defendant
Doxin, Doxin and Squiban, L.L.P.

11-30-11
Date

IN THE UNITED STATES DISTRICT COURT
FOR THE NORTHERN DISTRICT OF NEW COLUMBIA

John Madden, et. al.   )
    Plaintiff   )
)

        v.   )
                              No. 01-27255

)
Lifecord, Inc., et. al.   )
    Defendant   )

_____)

PLAINTIFF'S LIST
OF EXPERT WITNESSES

Pursuant to the Scheduling Order, dated September 25, 2011, John Madden, et. al., Plaintiff, sets forth below his list of expert witnesses.

1. <u>Mark G. Weingaarten, M.D.</u>

Position: Professor of Medicine, Harvey Medical School and Physician, Bowden Hospital.

Summary of Testimony: Dr. Weingaarten will testify that the procedures and process followed by the Defendant were materially deficient from that promised by the Defendant, and were not in accordance with industry practice.

2. <u>Chris D. Falsgraft, M.D.</u>

Position: Associate Professor of Medicine, New Columbia State Medical School, Assistant Director, Biochemistry, and consultant to Hamden Hospital.

Summary of Testimony: Dr. Falsgraft will testify that the process for preparing the stem cells was materially different from that described in the scientific literature, resulting in a defective design.

3. <u>Randal T. Kramer, Ph.D.</u>

   Position: Professor of Bioengineering, New Columbian State University, and Consultant to Lifecord, Inc. in Bellville, New Columbia.

   Summary of Testimony: Dr. Kramer will testify that the facilities were not adequate to ensure the safety of the stem cells, and that the facilities were materially deficient from industry practice.

4. <u>B. Jan Cummings, M.D.</u>

   Position: Director of the Lifecord Center, Bellville, New Columbia, Adjunct Professor, University of New Columbia, Department of Virology.

   Summary of Testimony: Dr. Cummings will testify to the industry practice in obtaining informed consent, breach of contract and the procedures to prepare the stem cells, and the Defendant's representation of their operation.

5. <u>Susan M. Consteria, Ph.D.</u>

   Position: Professor of Economics, University of New Columbia; and President of the National Economics Association.

   Summary of Testimony: Dr. Consteria will testify to the amount of damages for the loss of the stem cells, the conversion of the stem cells and for the breach of contract by the Defendant.

Submitted by:

Carole Cochran   11-20-2011
_____   _____
Carole Cochran, Esq.   Date
New Columbia Bar No. 698098
Attorney for the plaintiff

1
2
3
4
5
6
7
8
9
10
11
12
13
14
15

X. Deposition Excerpts

1

1
2
3
4
5
6
7
8
9
0

X.(A) Expert Witness Depositions

1

1   DEPOSITION
2   of
3   SAMUEL ABRAMOWITZ, M.D.
4
5   Deposition of Samuel Abramowitz, M.D., held at the Gordon Building, Bristol, New Columbia,
6   on the 15th day of December 2011, commencing at 10:00am.
7
8   Samuel Abramowitz, M.D., having been called as a witness, being duly sworn, testified as
9   follows:
10
11 **********
12
13 Q: Let=s talk a moment about your procedure which you published in 1997. Dr.
14 Abramowitz, you wrote about the use of adenovirus mediated transfer of interferon to stem cells,
15 identified as CD34+ cells, which are administered to the recipient in a process called gene
16 therapy. Is that basically what you did?
17
18 A: Not exactly. The use of adenovirus was published in 1997, as the first successful attempt
19 to introduce interferon directly into the patient=s tissue. The virus in its natural life cycle
20 invades a cell and takes with it its RNA which replicates in the host cell, which takes on its
21 genetic code. It is here that the interferon, which interferes with cancer cells, begins to destroy
22 leukemia cells.
23
24 Q: So, Dr. Abramowitz, the use of the adenovirus is simply as a vehicle to get the interferon
25 to the place where it can do the job of killing the leukemia?
26
27 A: Exactly. That is why it is called adenovirus mediated transfer.
28
29 Q: But, Dr. Abramowitz, I see that you published another paper in 1999 with some other
30 authors which discusses the same procedure, except you are using another virus? Would you
31 care to examine this article?
32
33 A: Yes.
34 [Witness examines article]
35
36 A: This paper discusses the use of retrovirus for the introduction of interferon into stem
37 cells. We found that the retroviruses were also effective at mediated transfer of interferon,
38 however, they also had some drawbacks.
39
40 Q: What were the benefits of the retroviruses?
41
42 A: The retroviruses were useful because they had much longer lives than the short 3-5
43 week lifespan of the adenoviruses. We found that the adenovirus, which is the family of viruses
44 which causes the common cold, had a very short life, and died out in about 3-5 weeks.
45 **********
46

1
2

DEPOSITION
OF
SAMUEL J. MESELSON, M.D.

1
2
3
4
5 Deposition of Samuel J. Meselson, M.D., held at the University of Bellville, New Columbia, on
6 the 16th day of December 2011, commencing at 10:00am.
7
8 Samuel J. Meselson, M.D., having been called as a witness, being duly sworn, testified as
9 follows:
10 *****************
11 Q: Would you please state your name and your title for the record?
12
13 A: My name is Dr. Samuel J. Meselson, I am a medical doctor and Professor of Medicine, at
14 the University of Bellville, New Columbia.
15
16 Q: Dr. Meselson, have you performed the procedure for the treatment of leukemia through
17 the use of virus-mediated stem cell transfer?
18
19 A: Yes, I have. Many times.
20
21 Q: About how many of these procedures would you say that you have done?
22
23 A: Probably 150 -200 in the last two years.
24
25 Q: How many of these are performed on behalf of Lifecord, Inc.?
26
27 A: I have developed a trusted relationship with Lifecord, Inc. and I am on their list of
28 physicians who do this procedure, so I don't know if you could say that I do these procedures on
29 behalf of Lifecord.
30
31 Q: Ok, Dr. Meselson, then how many of these procedures have you done as a result of being
32 listed as a physician by Lifecord?
33
34 A: Probably about 80% of the procedures that I have done.
35
36 Q: Dr. Meselson, what is your opinion concerning the quantity of the stem cells available for
37 treatment and the relationship with effectiveness of the treatment?
38
39 A: I have seen no correlation with the quantity of stem cells and the effectiveness of the
40 treatment.
41
42 Q: Can you explain that, please?
43
44 A: The preparation of the stem cells requires growing a large number of these stem cells by
45 multiplying the original material, thus it really doesn't matter how many stem cells you start

1   with, because you grow as many duplicate cells as needed. I almost always use the same amount
2   for the procedure.
3
4   Q: What is the quantity of the stem cells that you use?
5
6   A: You mean on average?
7
8   Q: Yes, exactly.
9
10   A: I would say that on average I use about 4.0×10^5/kg.
11
12   Q: If you use the same amount for the procedure each time, Dr. Meselson, how can you
13   conclude that different amounts do not affect the outcome?
14
15   A: Oh, simply that I have, in fact, used varying amounts in the past, but I have now begun to
16   use a uniform dose of stem cells.
17
18   Q: Why have you started using this uniform dose, Dr. Meselson? Are you relying upon
19   medical publications for this practice?
20
21   A: No, not really. I am relying upon my on experience and practice.
22
23   Q: Do you have any publications on this?
24
25   A: No I don't.
26   ....
27

<pre>
 1   DEPOSITION
 2   Of
 3   B. JAN CUMMINGS, Ph.D.
 4
 5   Deposition of B. Jan Cummings, M.D., held at the Jespers Building, Bristol, New Columbia, on
 6   the 17th day of December 2011, commencing at 2:00pm.
 7
 8   B. Jan Cummings, M.D., having been called as a witness, being duly sworn, testified as follows:
 9   **************
</pre>

■■

<pre>
10   Doxin: I would like to now turn to the issue of the representations of Lifecord. I would
11   like   to show you a copy of the webpage of Lifecord.
12
13   [Attorney shows witness document and witness examines the document.]
14
15   Witness: This is the website for Lifecord?
16
17   Doxin: Yes. Have you seen this before?
18
19   Witness: I don=t recall ever seeing their website, except the Madden=s attorney, Ms.
20   Cochran, showed me the part of the webpage which described the facilities of
21   Lifecord..
22
23   Doxin   :   And what did Ms. Cochran ask you about that webpage?
24
25   Cochran: Objection, that is privileged.
26
27   Doxin: The witness has opened the door, and I would like an answer.
28
29   Cochran: [to witness] I am advising you that you do not have to answer that.
30
31   Doxin: Alright, Dr. Cummings, in reference to the webpage I have before you, has
32   Lifecord suggested anything that is not true for banking umbilical cord blood?
33
34   Witness: Well, the long list of diseases which can be cured by stem cells is a bit of an
35   exaggeration. These are all diseases which are being researched for gene
36   therapy, but there are no guaranteed cures for these diseases.
37
38   Doxin: So, this list is an accurate list of diseases which <u>might</u> be cured using stem
39   cells.
40
41   Witness: Possibly, but it is not at all certain. Largely speculative.
42
43   Doxin: Dr. Cummings, you are the director of the Life Cord, Inc. umbilical cord blood
44   bank, are you not?
45   Witness: Yes, I am.
</pre>

1
2 Doxin: Then you obviously believe in the benefits of banking umbilical cord blood, do
3   you not?
4
5 Witness: Yes.
6
7 Doxin: Then, would you say that umbilical cord blood is always a recommended
8   therapy for leukemia?
9
10 Witness: Yes.
11
12 Doxin: Is there any disagreement in the field on this issue?
13
14 Witness: No, there is not.
15
16 **************
17 Doxin: Do you have an opinion about the quantity of stem cells necessary to   effectively
18   treat leukemia?
19
20 Witness: Yes, I do.
21
22 Doxin: What is that opinion?
23
24 Witness: There is a certain quantity of stem cells over which studies have shown the
25   gene therapy to be effective.
26
27 Doxin: What is that quantity?
28
29 Witness: The quantity of stem cells which correlate with a probability of survival of the
30   patient is usually over $2.2 \times 10\text{-}5\text{/kg}$ dose. But specifically, the survival
31   probability increases with the quantity of the stem cell dose. In other
32   words, the greater the quantity of stem cells, the greater the likelihood of
33   survival.
34
35 Doxin: Do you know the quantity of stem cells given to John Madden?
36
37 Witness: No, I do not.
38
39 Doxin: If I told you that the amount was $0.5 \times 10\text{-}5 \text{ /kg}$, would you have an opinion as
40   to whether this was a sufficient dose?
41
42 Witness: Based on studies done at the University of Minnesota, I would say that this was
43   far below what would be expected to be an effective dose.

DEPOSITION
of
RANDAL T. KRAMER, Ph.D.

Deposition of Randal T. Kramer Ph.D., held at New Columbia State University, Bellville, New Columbia, on the 19th day of December 2011, commencing at 9:00am.

Randal T. Kramer, Ph.D., having been called as a witness, being duly sworn, testified as follows:

****

Q: Have you seen the Lifecord storage unit, Dr. Kramer?

A: Yes, I have.

Q: Are these photographs of the storage unit where John Madden=s umbilical cord blood   stem cells were stored?

[Attorney shows witness photograph]

A: Yes, they appear to be.

Q: Are these typical storage units for the industry?

A: Actually, those units are about ten years old. There are much newer units being used, now.

Q: But do you mean to say that they are not acceptable for the industry?

A: No, they are just old.

Q: Are nitrogen tanks typically used in the industry for freezing the stem cells?

A: Yes.

Q: Are nitrogen tanks used by Lifecord?

A: Yes.

Q: Do you have an opinion as to whether they used the nitrogen tanks properly?

A: Yes, but they had no back up tanks.
****

1

1
2
3
4
5
6
7
8
9
10
11
12
13
14
15

X.(B) Parties and Fact Witness Depositions

1

Deposition of Skyler Sorenson, M.D., held at the offices of Lifecord, Inc., Bellville, New
Columbia, on the 21st day of December 2011, commencing at 12:00noon.

Skyler Sorenson, M.D., having been called as a witness, being duly sworn, testified as follows:

****

Q: Dr. Sorenson, would you please state your name and give us your title for the record.

A: I am Dr. Skyler Sorenson, Vice President for Research for Lifecord, Inc. and I am an
Adjunct Professor in the School of Medicine, University of Bellville, New Columbia.

Q: What is it that would make a company sell the stem cells that are the property of a
client with whom you have contracted to another person, without their permission? Is that
something that is done in your industry?

A: The Maddens had failed to make their payment in performance of the contract with
Lifecord. Once the Maddens breached their contract, the stem cells were no longer their
property. Companies need to recover their losses someway, and selling the stem cells to
someone who wanted them was one way to do that. It is done all the time in this industry.

Q: Is the practice in the industry to inquire of the client if they intend to fulfill their
payment obligation?

A: If someone fails to make a payment then they have breached their contract and it is
not necessary to consult with them further.

Q: Stem cells are a pretty important property, and there aren=t any more of them, isn=t
that correct, Dr. Sorenson?

A: Of course stem cells are important. Whether they are property or not is another
question. I think you could answer that yourself, Ms. Cochran.

Q: This is a deposition to ask questions of you, Dr. Sorenson. O.k., I would like to show
you a set of photos, Dr. Sorenson. Do you recognize these photos?

[Attorney shows document to witness]

A: Yes, these appear to be photographs of the collection procedure used on John
Madden. The last photo is the storage unit where the umbilical cord blood stem cells are stored.

Q: As Vice President for Research, Dr. Sorenson, did you make the selection for which

1 virus-mediated transfer mechanism that you would use?
2
3 A: Yes, I make all of the scientific research decisions.
4
5 Q: Why did you select an adenovirus-mediated transfer of interferon?
6
7 A: That's the industry standard, and has been in use for some years.
8
9 Q: Were you aware that the retrovirus-mediated transfer was much more dependable and
10 successful?
11
12 A: I was aware that they were doing research using retrovirus-mediated transfer, but I did not
13 think that it was advanced enough to switch our procedure.
14
15 Q: But isn't it true, Dr. Sorenson, that you have had a high percentage of failures using
16 adenovirus-mediated transfer because the virus dies too quickly, before it can get the job done?
17
18 A: I wouldn't say that.
19
20 Q: What is your success rate with treatments with your stem cell adenovirus-mediated
21 transfer product?
22
23 A: I don't know that I would call it a "product", but if you mean the process, I would say we
24 have about a 50% success rate, which is considered very good in the industry.
25
26 Q: Thank you, Dr. Sorenson.
27
28 **********
29

DEPOSITION
of
LOREN McCAFFERY, Ph.D.

1
2
3
4
5 Deposition of Loren McCaffery, Ph.D., held at the Lifecord Center, Bellville, New Columbia, on
6 the 20st day of December 2011, commencing at 2:00p.m.
7
8 Loren McCaffery, Ph.D., having been called as a witness, being duly sworn, testified as follows:
9
10 Q: Could I ask you to state your name for the record, and your position with Lifecord, Inc.?
11
12 A: My name is Loren McCaffery, and I am the Director of the Lifecord Center.
13
14 Q: Could you tell us about your educational background?
15
16 A: Yes, I have a Ph.D. in Microbiology from the University of Bellville and I did a Post-Doc
17 at the Jedah University School of Medicine.
18
19 Q: Why would you take the stem cells preserved for an infant and sell them to an estranged
20 aunt --- someone whom you have never met before --- without even once picking up the phone to
21 contact the Maddens?
22
23 A: We no longer had a contract with the Maddens. This was a procedure that was part of the
24 contractual agreement upon default. The Maddens had made six monthly payments but defaulted
25 on the seventh payment, their final payment.
26
27 Q: Did you have any reason to believe that the Maddens were ending their contract with you
28 since they had made all of their other payments in a timely manner ?
29
30 A: No, but this is not the first time this has happened with customers.
31
32 Q: On what date was the final payment due?
33
34 A: I believe it was June 15, 2011.
35
36 Q: When did you receive a call from Jerry Madden's estranged aunt, Sarah Whitting?
37
38 A: On June 16, 2011.
39
40 Q: How did Ms. Whitting know that you had the infant's stem cells in your possession?
41
42 A: She had heard from the family that they were using Lifecord as insurance against their
43 own child potentially inheriting the genetic tendency to develop leukemia, because the aunt, Ms.
44 Whitting had the disease.
45

1   Q: What did you say to Ms. Whitting?
2
3   A: I told her that I would have to get back with her to see what the Maddens would like to do
4   with the stem cells.
5
6   Q: And what did Ms. Whitting say at that point?
7
8   A: She told me that the Maddens had given her permission to take some of the stem cells,
9   and that she didn't want to take all of them, but she knew that this was her only hope of curing
10   her leukemia.
11
12   Q: Did you call the Maddens to confirm this conversation or report it to anyone else in the
13   company?
14
15   A: No, I assumed Ms. Whitting was telling me the truth, and it seemed to fit with the fact
16   that the Madden's had stopped making payments on the stem cells.
17
18   Q: Did you transfer the stem cells to Ms. Whitting?
19
20   A: Yes, we did.
21
22   Q: How much did you charge Ms. Whitting for the stem cells and the transfer?
23
24   A: $2500.
25
26   Q: That was $2500 you would not have made if the infant Conrad Madden had never needed
27   the stem cells, is that correct?
28
29   A: Not necessarily. We collect an annual fee of $250 a year, which could add up to $2500.
30
31   Q: But you had no question about notifying the parents, Jerry and Sally Madden about this
32   transaction?
33
34   A: No, because the Maddens had ceased to make payments.
35
36   ****************
37

DEPOSITION
of
JERRY MADDEN

Deposition of Jerry Madden, plaintiff, held at the Law Offices of Carole Cochran, Bellville, New Columbia, on the 22nd day of December 2011, commencing at 2:00p.m.

Jerry Madden, having been called as a witness, being duly sworn, testified as follows:

Q: Could you please state your name for us for the record, sir?

A: Jerry Madden.

Q: Mr. Madden, we are very sorry about the death of your son, Conrad, and we are very sorry to have to ask you these sensitive questions, but if you will bear with us, we will try to get through this as quickly as possible.

A: It would be better if you could have been as interested in our son a couple of months ago.

[Attorney for Jerry Madden asks to go off the record; Attorney and Jerry Madden leave the room, and return a few minutes later.]

Q: Mr. Madden, do you remember talking with our Director, Dr. Loren McCaffrey, concerning the use of Lifecord as a system for preserving stem cells from the umbilical cord of your child which had not yet been born?

A: Yes.

Q: Do you remember the discussion of the terms of the agreement? That is, if you decide to discontinue the service that the company, Lifecord, could dispose of the stem cells?

A: No, I don't remember discussing this.

Q: Did Dr. McCaffrey go over the enrollment agreement with you?

A: Yes.

Q: About how much time would you say she spent going over the enrollment agreement?

A: About an hour.

Q: Did you have any questions for her during that time?

A: Not that I remember.

1   Q: Do you recall asking Dr. McCaffrey about the payments, and asking if you could have a
2   discount for the service?
3
4   A: I could have made a comment like that.
5
6   Q: Do you have an aunt, Ms. Whitting?
7
8   A: Yes, she is my aunt.
9
10   Q: Did you ever tell Ms. Whitting about your plan to store stem cells for your son, Conrad
11   Madden?
12
13   A: I did not tell her. I told my other aunt, Rebecca Madden.
14
15   Q: Does your aunt, Ms. Whitting, have leukemia?
16
17   A: Yes, she does.
18
19   Q: When you made your last payment to Lifecord, Mr. Madden, did you use registered mail
20   or return receipt services, or any other method to ensure that your payment reached the defendant,
21   Lifecord?
22
23   A: No. I never had a problem before.
24
25   Q: So you have no way to verify that you made the payment to Lifecord?
26
27   A: I mailed the payment on June 11, 2011 and it should have arrived on June 15, 2011.
28   Besides, we have a 45 day period of the due date to make any payment that is due.
29
30   Q: When did you finally make that June 15, 2011 payment, Mr. Madden?
31
32   A: We didn't know that Lifecord had not received the payment, and didn't find out until
33   September 7, when we called the scumbags to request our stem cells, right after we found that
34   little Conrad had leukemia.
35
36   Q: When did you find that Conrad had leukemia, Mr. Madden?
37
38   A: On August 30, 2011.
39
40   Q: Did the payment that you purportedly mailed to Lifecord, ever show up in the mail?
41
42   A: Yes, the envelope came back, undeliverable to our address September 10, 2011.
43
44   Q: Is this a copy of the check that was returned?
45

1   A: Yes, it is.
2
3   Q: Do you write all of your checks in the order of their numbers, that is, consecutively?
4
5   A: Yes, of course.
6
7   Q: Did you sign the enrollment agreement?
8
9   A: I think so.
10
11
12   *****************
13
14

1

DEPOSITION
of
ALEX HENLEY, M.D.

1
2
3
4
5   Deposition of Alex Henley, M.D., held at the Hillhouse Hospital, New Columbia, on the 12th
6   day of December 2011, commencing at 2:00p.m.
7
8   Alex Henley M.D., having been called as a witness, being duly sworn, testified as follows:
9
10 Q: Could you please state your name and your occupation for the record?
11
12 A: I am Dr. Alex Henley, practicing physician in New Columbia.
13
14 Q: Did you recommend that the plaintiff, Jerry Madden contact Lifecord and arrange to store
15 stem cells from their yet unborn son?
16
17 A: I discussed the possibility with him, yes.
18
19 Q: And Dr. Henley, can you tell us why you recommended Lifecord to the plaintiff, Jerry
20 Madden?
21
22 A: I knew from Jerry's health information disclosure that he had an aunt with leukemia, and
23 it could possibly be hereditary.
24
25 Q: Would the use of stem cells in a child that developed leukemia be important?
26
27 A: Absolutely. It could be lifesaving.
28
29 Q: Is there any other reason that you would have recommended Lifecord to Mr. Madden?
30
31 A: I have worked with Lifecord for the five years that they have been in business, and they
32 seem to be a good company.
33
34 Q: You don't have any financial interest in Lifecord, do you Dr. Henley?
35
36 A: I had stock in the company which Dr. Sorenson gave to me when they first organized in
37 exchange for my advice, but I have since sold the stock.
38
39 Q: Why did you sell it?
40
41 A: I just don't like keeping up with the reports and filing the tax forms. It's not worth the
42 hassle.
43
44 Q: How much did you sell the stock for?
45

1   A: Not much. Probably $5,000.
2
3   Q: Ok, Dr. Henley, would you say that Lifecord has been a dependable company and would
4   you recommend it again?
5
6   A: Yes, absolutely. They are providing an invaluable service.
7
8   Q: Thank you Dr. Henley.
9   **********************

XI. Exhibits File

Resume

Samuel Abramowitz, M.D.

Educational Background

Internal Medicine, Diplomate, 1985.

Internship, Immunology, Naval Hospital, Bethesda, Maryland (1976-79).

M.D., Hampton University, Westport, New York, graduated with honors in 1975.

B.S., Chemistry, Stanford University, Palo Alto, California, graduated with high honors in 1970.

Experience

Professor of Medicine, New Columbia Medical School, Chair of the Immunology Department, Brigham & Bondary's Hospital, Washington, New Columbia. (2005 - present).

Chief , Department of Immunology, West Haven University Hospital, West Haven, NH (2000-2005).

RESUME

B. Jan Cummings, Ph.D.

Educational Background

Postdoctoral Research, Avery University, Charles City, Virginia (1991-94).

Ph.D., Virology, Hardins University, Bellville, New Columbia, graduated in 1990. Dissertation: "The Statistical Associations between Viral Vectors and Host Cell Survival in Various Transportation Solutions."

M.S., Virology, Saint Paul University, Bowie City, Indiana (1985).

B.S., Chemistry, with honors, University of Texas, San Jose, Texas (1981).

Experience

Director, LifeCord, Inc., an umbilical cord blood stem cell processing and storage company.

Adjunct Professor, Department of Virology, University of New Columbia, Bellville, New Columbia (1999-present)

Senior Research Associate, Lifecord Center, Inc., Bellville, New Columbia (2000-2002).

Teaching Fellow, Avery University, Charles City, Virginia (1995-1998).

Resume

Samuel Meselson, M.D.

Academic Background

M.D., University of Kansas, Kansas City, Kansas graduated with honors (1980).

M.S., Toxicology, University of Kansas, Kansas City, Kansas, thesis, "The Exposure of Titanium Dioxide to Mice and the Incidence of Liver Malformations." (1976).

B.A., English, with a minor in Chemistry, Franklin College, Birmington, Massachusetts (1973).

Experience

Vice President for Research, LifeCord, Inc.

Adjunct Professor, Department of Immunology, University of Bellville, Bellville, New Columbia, Harvey Medical School (1995 - present)

Senoir Physician, Bowden Hospital, teaching hospital of the Harvey Medical School (1995 - present).

Professor of Medicine, University of Tennessee, School of Medicine, Nashville, Tennessee (1985-1995).

Internship, Internal Medicine, Valapariso University, Sumter, North Dakota (1980-1985).

CURRICULUM VITAE

Randal T. Kramer, Ph.D.

Education

Postdoctoral Research, University of Cleveland, Cleveland, Ohio (2000-2005).

Ph.D., Civil Engineering, University of California, San Juan, California. Dissertation, "The Structural Strength of Depleted Underground Storage Tanks." (2000).

M.S., Civil Engineering, University of California, San Juan, California. (1995).

B.S., Biochemistry, Rowe University, Cincinnati, Ohio (1991).

Professional Experience

Professor, Department of Bioengineering, New Columbian State University (2005 - present).

Staff Engineer, Engineering Life, Inc., Bellville, New Columbia (2006- present).

The New York Times

December 1, 1998

The Hope, and Hype, of Cord Blood

By DENISE GRADY

Should parents pay a blood bank to store the blood from their newborn baby's umbilical cord and placenta, in case that child or another family member ever needs it to treat cancer or leukemia?

Expectant parents are being urged to do so by companies that have sprung up during the past few years to sell cord-blood banking as a form of "biological insurance" against such dreaded diseases. The pitch is based on reports in medical journals, such as a major study published last week in the New England Journal of Medicine, showing that cord blood can sometimes be used in place of a bone marrow transplant.

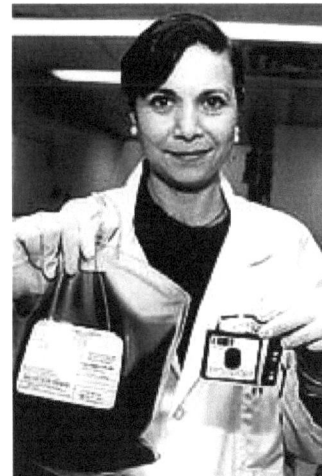

Courtesy of the New York Blood Center

Dr. N. Ludy Dobrila of the New York Blood Center contrasted the amount of bone marrow used in an operation, left, with the amount of cord blood needed.

Like bone marrow, cord blood is rich in stem cells, which can churn out many different types of cells to rebuild a patient's blood supply and immune system after high doses of radiation and chemotherapy. And a patient's own cord blood, or that from a relative, is more likely than cord blood from an unrelated donor to be a good tissue match and to be accepted by the recipient's body.

Some experts in bone-marrow transplantation and blood banking frown on the cord-blood business, arguing that people are being frightened into wasting money on a service they will probably never need. Moreover, private companies are growing in tandem with public banks, and some scientists worry that private banking will limit public access to cord blood. They are concerned because the cord blood in private banks remains the property of the donor family and is not available to patients seeking a compatible donor.

But the companies say that however remote the possibility that the blood will be needed, people who choose to bank their own cord blood have a right to do so. In most cases their cord blood would be thrown away in the delivery room if they did not pay to bank it. There are only a few cord-blood banks in the United States, and most hospitals do not have specially trained staff members to collect the blood.

Like bone marrow, cord blood must be matched to the recipient by tests for six inherited traits that determine an individual's tissue type. Cord blood does not have to be as precisely matched as bone marrow, but still, the closer the match, the better the odds of success. The weaker the match, the more likely it is that the recipient's body will reject the transplant, or the transplant will attack the recipient's tissues, in a life-threatening reaction called graft versus host disease.

The companies that freeze cord blood and bank it point out that a person's own cord blood is a perfect match, and a sibling's cord blood a more likely match than a specimen from a stranger. And so, the argument goes, the best way to protect an entire family from the unthinkable is to save the newborns' cord blood.

Promotional literature for one company, Cord Blood Registry, in San Bruno, Calif., emphasizes that people with cancer in the family may have a special interest in cord-blood banking, along with those who have the hardest time finding matches, which includes members of racial minorities, especially families in which the parents are of different races.

According to a spokeswoman, Scoti Kaesshaefer, the company reaches parents-to-be by promoting itself to doctors, nurses and childbirth educators, and by leaving information at hospitals. Among the promotional materials the company provided to the New York Times were copies of articles from other newspapers suggesting that cancer among children is on the rise. The company also has a Web site and an 800 number with a recorded greeting that instructs callers to have their credit cards ready.

The idea of saving one's own cord blood seems to be catching on. Cord Blood Registry, which describes itself as the largest private cord-blood banking firm in the United States, has stored 10,000 samples during the past three years: 1,500 in 1995, 3,000 in 1996 and 6,000 in 1997. The company charges an initial fee of $1,200 to collect a sample and freeze it, and then $95 a year to keep it stored in liquid nitrogen at the blood bank at the University of Arizona. Customers include people with perfectly healthy children, who just want extra peace of mind, as well as some families who have lost a child to leukemia or another disease and fear for the health of their other children.

In its three years of operation, eight customers have retrieved their cord blood for use in medical treatment, said Kaesshaefer. All eight samples were used for siblings or relatives, she said. By contrast, the largest public-access bank of cord blood, at the New York Blood Center in Manhattan, has collected only 8,686 specimens in six years. But nearly 800 of those samples have been used to treat patients, many of them children, in the United States and overseas.

Critics of private cord-blood companies point out that even if a person with banked cord blood does need a transplant later, the stored blood may not be the best choice. Dr. Pablo Rubinstein, who directs the cord-blood program at the New York Blood Center, said there was a compelling medical argument against using a patient's own cord blood in some cases. In some young children with leukemia, he said, malignant cells were already present at birth in the cord blood, and transfusing those cells back into the child later might contribute to a relapse. In addition, he said, bone marrow from a donor could help destroy diseased cells, an effect known as graft versus leukemia. A person's own cord blood might not have that effect, and in some cases even a sibling's might not.

Dr. John Wagner, associate director of bone marrow transplantation at the University of Minnesota in Minneapolis, said that for a child being treated recently, he deliberately rejected cord blood from a sibling in favor of a well-matched unit from an unrelated donor, hoping to take advantage of its antileukemic effect.

Dr. Robertson Parkman, director of bone marrow transplantation at Children's Hospital in Los Angeles, said he saw no point in banking cord blood for most families. "It's motivated by fear," he said.

But in families with an ill child who might need a bone-marrow transplant, he said, it makes sense to collect cord blood from any siblings born later and save it. Medical centers with transplant programs will often perform that service, he said.

So will some of the private companies, without a fee. When a bone-marrow donor could not be found for 4-year-old Joshua Kelton, who was suffering from leukemia, his parents, stationed at a military base in Honolulu, conceived another child in the hope that the baby's tissues would match Joshua's. They did, and Cord Blood Registry collected the cord blood at birth, stored it in Arizona for a month, and then, when Joshua was ready for the procedure, transported it to a medical center at Stanford University. Joshua was treated with his infant brother's cord blood in August, and has been declared free of leukemia.

"Right now, he's 100 percent," his father said in a telephone interview, "a normal child, the way he was before this happened."

But the Keltons' experience is hardly representative. That the family was certain it would need the cord blood sets it apart from most families that store the blood. Wagner is wary of the hard sell of some of the cord-blood companies. "My concern is that it be presented fairly to expectant mothers, who are already fairly vulnerable," he said. "I have a lot of obstetricians and parents calling me and complaining it's too late, they missed the opportunity. Others call saying, 'Should I do this?' It's hard to answer. I don't want to bias them. We have someone now who takes the calls for me because it got to be overwhelming."

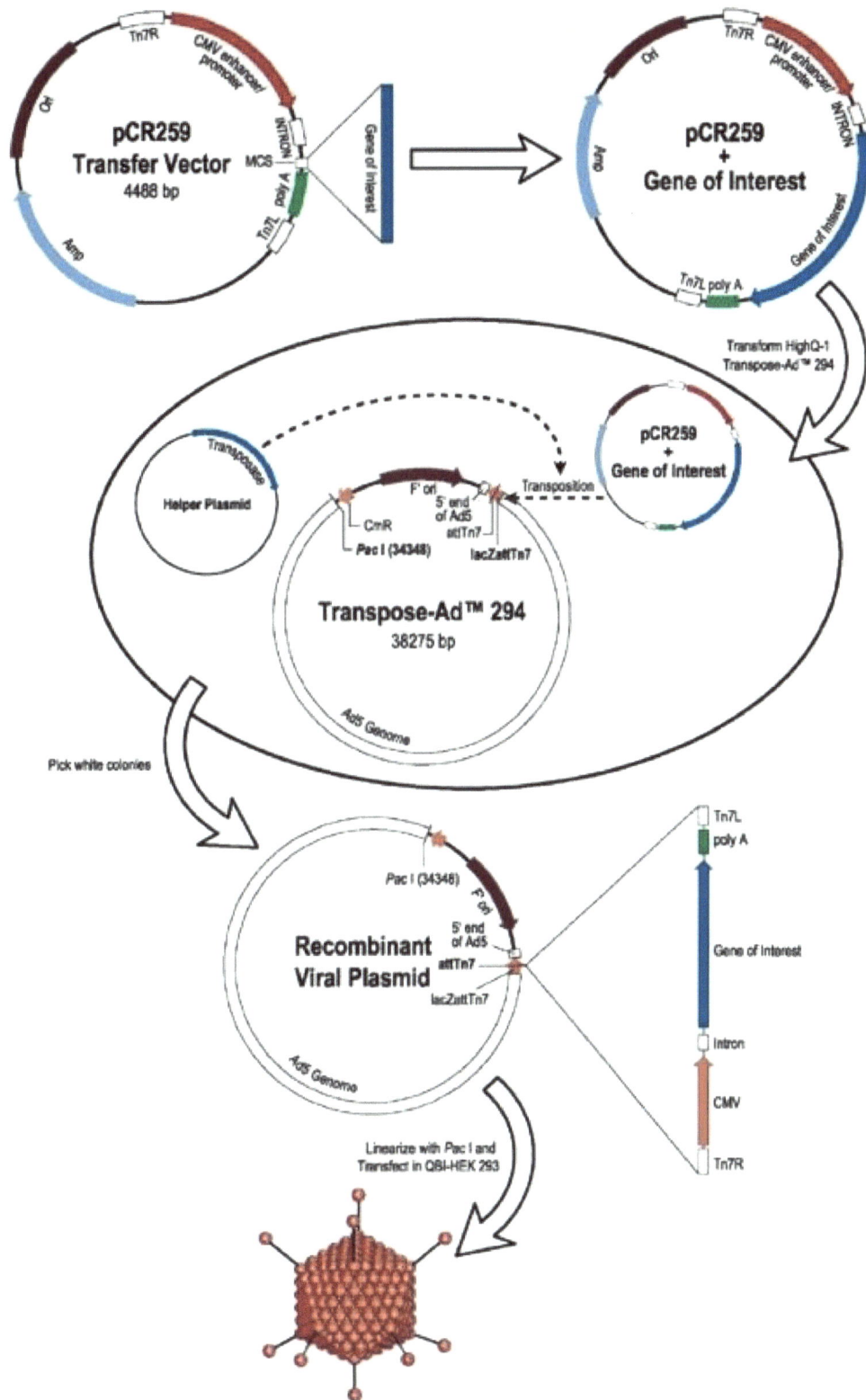

Figure 1: Generation of Recombinant Adenoviruses Using the Transpose-Ad™ System

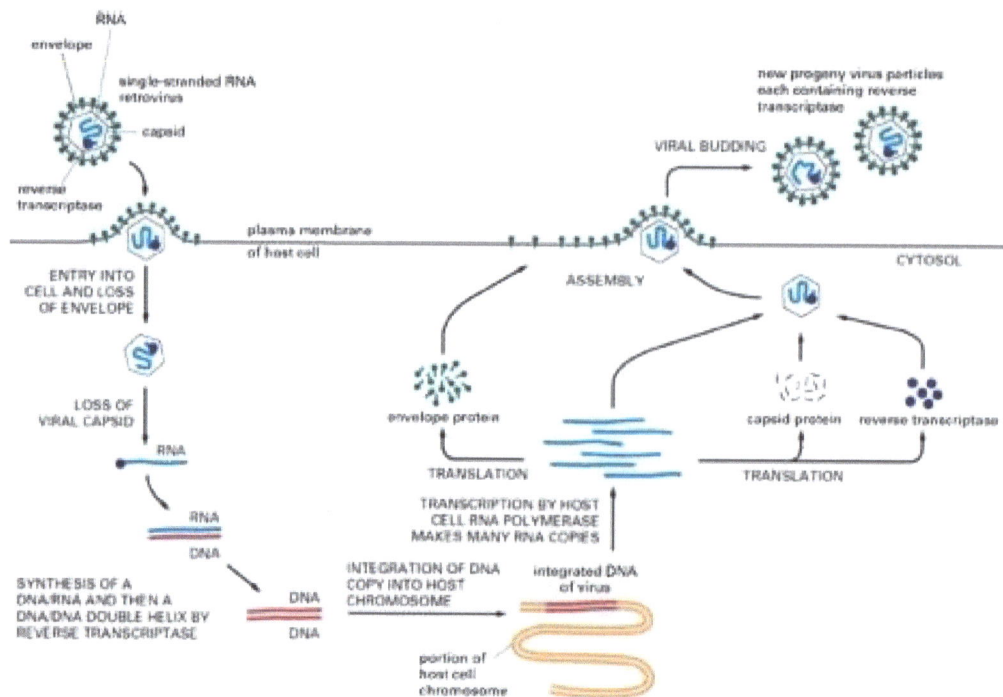

Life Cycle of a Retrovirus

Legend:

The typical retrovirus genome consists of a single-stranded RNA of about 8500 nucleotides. The enzyme reverse transcriptase is a multifunctional enzyme that first makes a DNA copy of the viral RNA molecule. It then acts as a nuclease to remove the RNA, and then makes a second DNA strand, generating a double-stranded DNA copy of the RNA genome. The integration of this DNA into the host chromosome, catalyzed by a viral protein called integrase, is required for the synthesis of new viral RNA molecules by the host cell RNA polymerase. Retroviruses are examples of enveloped viruses, in which the protein shell is further enclosed by an outer lipid bilayer membrane. The envelope contains proteins that enable the virus to bind to cells, and that aid its entry into a cell. As indicated, the lipid membrane is acquired when the virus is released from the cell by a process of budding from the plasma membrane, taking some of the plasma membrane with it. The budding process is reversed when the virus reinfects a cell.

From:
Bruce Alberts, Dennis Bray, Alexander Johnson, Julian Lewis, Martin Raff, Keith Roberts and Peter Walter, *Essential Cell Biology: An Introductino to the Molecular Biology of the Cell* Garland Publishing, Taylor & Francis Group (1998).

MedicalLine Abstract

Adenovirus mediated alpha interferon (IFN-alpha)gene transfer into CD34+ cells and CML mononuclear cells

Stem Cell Journal 1997 Sept 5(3):459-485 (ISSN: 1044-6099)

Feinman D.; Abramowitz S.; Jackson P.; Hamid H.; Dorsaneo K.; Smith R. Department of Immunology, New Columbia Medical School, New Columbia 20200, USA

Gene transfer or gene therapy has advantages in the treatment of a variety of disorders due to its selective expression within specific mammalian cells. Interferon-alpha (IFN-alpha) has been used in the management of leukemia but is diverse adverse activities with multiple potential side effects, possibly unrelated to therapeutic targets, may negatively influence the ability of IFN-alpha to treat this disorder. Therefore, we examined the ability of adenovirus (Ad)-IFN-alpha gene construct to transfect normal (CD34+ cells) and chronic myelogenous leukemia (CML) bone marrow mononuclear cells (BMMNC) and the transient overexpression of IFN-alpha in these cells. Ad-cytomegalovirus promoter driven IFN-alpha (AdCMV-IFN-alpha) at multiple doses was assessed to transfect highly prurified CD34+ cells in liquid culture, and optimal transduction of CD34+ cells was achieved using 120 plaque forming unites. Flow cytometric determinations revealed that there was no significant difference in cell viability for the 4 h or 24 h transfection periods. Immunoassay of IFN-alpha produced by CD34+ cells shows that IFN-alpha levels increased several fold in transfected cells. Transient expression of the IFN-alpha gene did not suppress proliferation of CD34+ progenitors as indicated by BFU-E or colony forming units-granulocyte-macrophage (CFU-GM) growth. Reverse transcriptase/polymerase chain reaction analysis of RNA from CD34+ harvested CFU-GM progenitor cells demonstrated transient IFN-alpha mRNA expression. Similarly, CML BMMNC were transfected with AdCMV-IFN-alpha under similar conditions as described for CD34+ cells. BMMNC were transfected with AdCMV-IFN-alpha under similar conditions as described for CD34+ cells. BMMNC cells exposed to adenovirus for 24 h and 48 h were found to express IFN-alpha at a substnatial level. This in vitro data suggest that Ad-mediated gene trassnfer of IFN-alpha into hematopoietic stem cells can be achieved and that the IFN-alpha gene can be translated into its specific mRNA in CD34+ progenitor cells.

MedicalLine Abstract

Effect of retroviral-mediated IFN-alpha gene transfer on human erythroleukemic and CD34+ cell growth and differentiation is distinct

J. Stem Cell & Virology Research 1999 Nov;9(4):671-692 (ISSN: 1744-9834)

Johnson E.; Feinman D.; Abramowitz S.; Wallace L; Hamid H.; Jenkins H.; Department of Immunology, New Columbia Medical School, New Columbia 20200, USA

Human interferon-alpha (IFN-alpha) has been used in the management of leukemia, but its diverse adverse effects may influence the abilitly of IFN-alpha to treat this disease. We developed two retroviral vectors, LSN-IFN-alpha and LNC-IFN-alpha, in which IFN-alpha cDNA was driven by viral LTR and CMV promoters, respectively. After transduction into the PA317 and PG13 retroviral packaging cells, high titers of retrovirus were produced and were used to infect K562 and human BM CD34+ hematopoietic cells. The IFN-alpha gene expression in transduced K562 cells was confirmed by Northern blot RT-PCR, RIA, and biologic assay. Cell proliferation and cell viability in IFN-alpha-transduced K562 cells were significanlty suppressed as compared with control K562 cells Although the IFN-alpha expression in K562 cells did not affect BCR/ABL expression, it apparently upregulated the production of adhesion molecules (VLA-4 and Mac-1). We evaluated the effect of IFN-alpha gene transfer on human CD34+ cells infected with LSN-IFN-transduced CD34+ cells produced 72.2+/-15 U/ml of IFN-alpha compared with 4.3+/-1.2 U/ml in control CD34+ cells. Methylcellulose clonogenic assay indicated that IFN-alpha-transduced CD34+ cells produced similar numbers of burst-forming units-erythrocytes (BFU-E)/colony-forming units-GM (CFU-GM) colonies as compared with control CD34+ cells. Selected colonies expressed IFN-alpha and neo7) mRNA, as measured by RT-PCR. These studies indicate that retrovirus-mediated IFN-alpha gene transfer may provide useful tool for studying the effect of IFN-alpha gene transfer on leukemic cells and long-lived CD34+ cells.

LifeCord Storage Unit and Work Area

Storage unit storing housing umbilical cord blood of John Madden from November 20, 2000 until September 15, 2001.

LifeCord Main Facility where cord blood stem cells are processed and stored.

Attachment P, Samuel Meselson deposition

View 1. Procedure used in the removal of umbilical cord blood from birth, from John Madden.

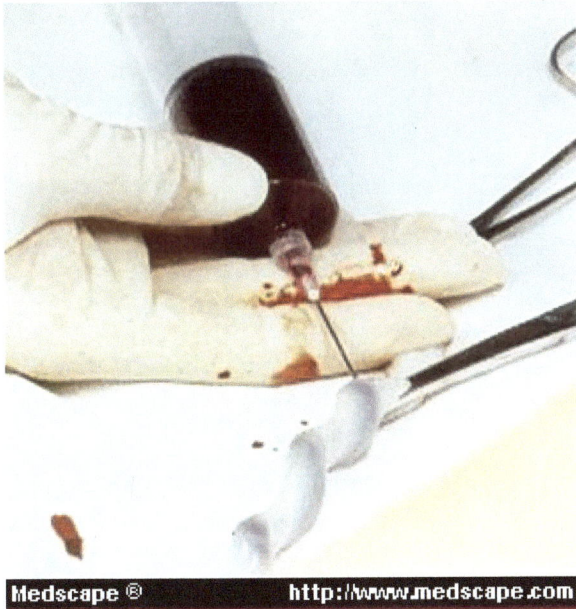

View 2. Procedure used in the removal of umbilical cord blood from birth, from John Madden.

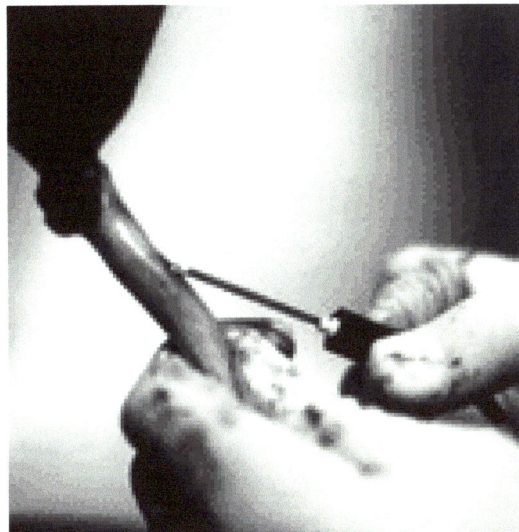

LifeCord, inc.

Congratulations.
You' re going to have a baby!
But what should you be doing to prepare, right now?

Home
Contact Us
Enrollment Forms
Checklist
Liability Forms
Medical Health
History

Why Preserve my baby's cord blood?

There are currently 75 diseases that can be treated with cord blood stem cells in the event of the development of one of these blood-related diseases. Studies have shown that a newborn has about a 1 in 300 chance of developing one of these diseases, and now LifeCord, Inc. can give your child a second chance. Cord blood storage is a once in a lifetime gift from parents that can be used throughout the child's life. We hope you will never need it, but if you do, we are here.

What are cord blood stem cells?

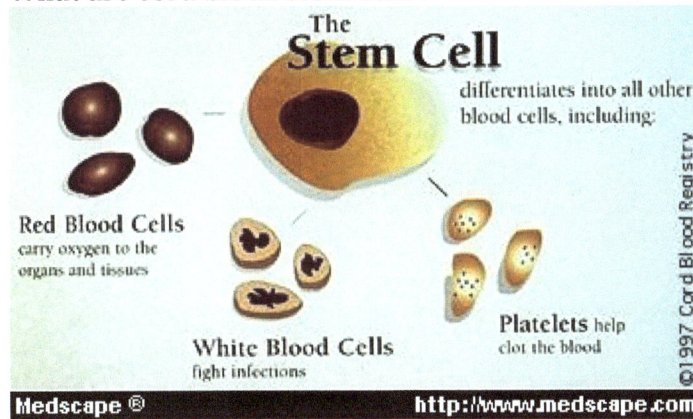

Cord blood stem cells are the most frequently used stem cells for the treatment of disease. The stem cells from umbilical cord blood are the most studied of all stem cells and are hematopoietic progenitors and can regenerate blood and immune system responses.
The cord blood is what remains in the umbilical cord after birth, after the cord is separated from the child. These cord blood stem cells are used to treat life-threatening diseases like leukemia, sickle cell anemia, blood and immune disorders and the damages of chemotherapy.

How are cord blood stem cells collected?

Your enrollment includes a cord blood collection kit and it takes only a few moments by your doctor or midwife to collect the stem cells. The process is non-invasive and does not interrupt the birthing process or bonding with mother and child.

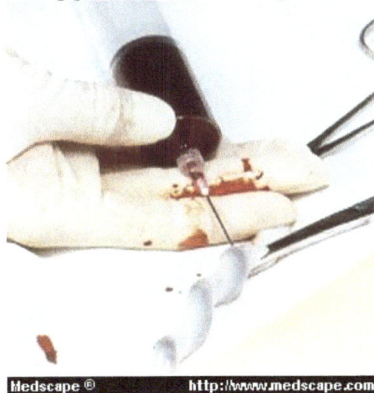

These are just a few of the 65+ diseases that can be treated with stem cells!

Acute Leukemias
Acute Biphenotypic Leukemia
Acute Lymphocytic Leukemia (ALL)
Acute Myelogenous Leukemia (AML)
Acute Undifferentiated Leukemia

Chronic Leukemias
Chronic Lymphocytic Leukemia (CLL)
Chronic Myelogenous Leukemia (CML)
Juvenile Chronic Myelogenous Leukemia (JCML)
Juvenile Myelomonocytic Leukemia (JMML)

Plasma Cell Disorders
Multiple Myeloma
Plasma Cell Leukemia
Waldenstrom's Macroglobulinemia

Other Malignancies
Brain Tumors
Breast Cancer
Ewing Sarcoma
Neuroblastoma
Ovarian Cancer
Renal Cell Carcinoma
Small-Cell Lung Cancer
Testicular Cancer

Autoimmune Diseases
Evan Syndrome
Multiple Sclerosis (Experimental)
Rheumatoid Arthritis (Experimental)
Systemic Lupus Erythematosus (Experimental)

Other Inherited Disorders
Cartilage-Hair Hypoplasia
Ceroid Lipofuscinosis
Congenital Erythropoietic Porphyria
Glanzmann Thrombasthenia
Lesch-Nyhan Syndrome
Osteopetrosis
Tay Sachs Disease

Phagocyte Disorders
Chediak-Higashi Syndrome
Chronic Granulomatous Disease
Neutrophil Actin Deficiency
Reticular Dysgenesis

Liposomal Storage Diseases
Adrenoleukodystrophy
Gaucher's Disease
Hunter's Syndrome (MPS-II)
Hurler's Syndrome (MPS-IH)
Krabbe Disease
Maroteaux-Lamy Syndrome (MPS-VI)
Metachromatic Leukodystrophy
Morquio Syndrome (MPS-IV)
Mucolipidosis II (I-cell Disease)
Mucopolysaccharidoses (MPS)
Niemann-Pick DiseaseSanfilippo Syndrome (MPS-III)
Sly Syndrome, Beta-Glucuronidase Deficiency (MPS-VII)
Wolman Disease

Histiocytic Disorders
Familial Erythrophagocytic
Lymphohistiocytosis
Hemophagocytosis
Histiocytosis-X

Langerhans' Cell Histiocytosis

Inherited Erythrocyte Abnormalities
Beta Thalassemia Major
Blackfan-Diamond Anemia
Pure Red Cell Aplasia
Sickle Cell Disease

Congenital (Inherited) Immune System Disorders
Absence of T & B Cells SCID
Absence of T Cells, Normal B Cell SCID
Ataxia-Telangiectasia
Bare Lymphocyte Syndrome
 Leukocyte Adhesion Deficiency
Omenn's Syndrome
Severe Combined Immunodeficiency (SCID)
SCID with Adenosine Deaminase Deficiency
Wiskott-Aldrich Syndrome
X-Linked Lymphoproliferative Disorder

Myelodysplastic Syndromes
Amyloidosis
Chronic Myelomonocytic Leukemia (CMML)
 Refractory Anemia with Excess Blasts (RAEB)
Refractory Anemia with Excess Blasts in Transformation (RAEB-T)
Refractory Anemia with Ringed Sideroblasts (RARS)

Stem Cell Disorders
Aplastic Anemia (Severe)
Congenital Cytopenia
Dyskeratosis Congenita
Fanconi Anemia
Paroxysmal Nocturnal Hemoglobinuria (PNH)

Myeloproliferative Disorders
Acute Myelofibrosis
Agnogenic Myeloid Metaplasia (Myelofibrosis)
Essential Thrombocythemia
Polycythemia Vera

Lymphoproliferative Disorders
Hodgkin's Disease
Non-Hodgkin's Lymphoma
Prolymphocytic Leukemia

Inherited Platelet Abnormalities
Amegakaryocytosis / Congenital
Thrombocytopenia

These are just some of the Potential Future Stem Cell Applications*
Alzheimer's Disease, Diabetes, Heart Disease, Liver Disease, Muscular Dystrophy, Parkinson's Disease
Spinal Cord Injury, and Stroke.

For questions about enrollment, please contact us at:
FAX is 1-800-324-3030, 24 hours a day, 7 days a week; or
MAIL is 3030 Elgin Lane, Hopesville, California 99890; or
DOWNLOAD these forms from www.lifecord.com and fax or mail completed forms.
If you have any questions, please do not hesitate to call us, and we will be happy to assist you.

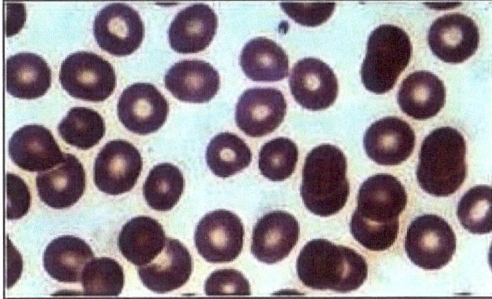

CORD BLOOD BANKS / Critics decry commercialism

Companies which store umbilical cords to use for future medical treatments for children are exploiting parents' fears, says critics of the new business of cord blood banks. Exaggerated claims are being made. One company in California displays on its website X-ray images of brain and breast cancers treated successfully with pluripotent stem cells, even though these are not the same as cord- blood stem cells.

In both the United States and Australia, public donor banks exist for umbilical cord blood, while private banks charge a hefty sign-up fee and an annual maintenance fee. But critics say that there is only a 1-in-10,000 chance that a child will develop a disease treatable with cord-blood cells and a one-in-four chance that the child will be able to use the cells. Promotions of the service are sometimes based on therapies that do not currently exist, and may never exist. Furthermore, cord blood may not even be viable after ten years of storage. -- *Wired News, Dec 20, 2001*

Bone marrow CD34+ cell dose correlates with transplant related mortality and survival in HLA identical sibling BMT for hematologic malignancies (Meeting abstract).

Abstract No: 888976334

Author(s):   L M Daniels, S Simmons, K Barlow

Abstract: The CD34+ cell dose of bone marrow allografts may be an important factor affecting transplant outcome. We describe the impact of CD34 cell dose on transplant related mortality (TRM) and define a threshold dose for optimum results. Twenty eight patients with hematologic malignancies including 14 CML chronic phase, 3 CML accelerated phase, 3 CML blast crisis, 3 MDS in transformation, 2 AML in relapse and 3 with multiple myeloma, received T-depleted BMT from HLA identical siblings. Patients with uncontrolled leukemia or marrow fibrosis were considered to have high disease risk. Depletion was carried out by elutriation. Post-transplant cyclosporine was given as additional GVHD prophylaxis. On day +30 and +45, patients without greater than or equal to grade II GVHD received lymphocyte transfusions from their donors to prevent leukemia relapse. CMV surveillance cultures and antigen detection was performed weekly and reactivation was treated with ganciclovir and IV Ig. The bone marrow CD34 cell dose was 2-3.8 x 10(6)/kg (5 patients), 1.06-1.6 (10 patients) and less than 1.0 (13 patients). In the first 6 months post-transplant, 11 patients died of whom 9 received less than 1.0 x 10(6) CD34 cells/kg. No patient receiving more than 2 X 10(6) CD34 cells/kg died. In an analysis of factors affecting outcome only the CD34+ cell dose correlated significantly with survival. Survival for 14 patients who received more than 1.0 x 10(6) CD34+ cells was 95% versus 40% (p less than 0.001) for 14 patients who received less. Age, disease risk, lymphocyte dose given and occurrence of grade II or more GVHD had no significant adverse effect on early TRM (2 relapse deaths excluded). Neutrophil and lymphocyte recovery was identical but monocyte recovery was earlier in the group given more than 2 x 10(6) CD34 cells. In addition these patients became red cell (p=0.07) and platelet (p=0.05) transfusion independent earlier, required less G-CSF administration during ganciclovir treatment (p=0.003) and stayed in the hospital fewer days (p=0.05) than the other patients. From the above results we conclude that 2 x 10(6) CD34+ cells/kg or more are required for optimum results in HLA identical sibling BMT.

Attachment 6, Cummings deposition

Rate of survival of umbilical cord stem cells in recipient in relation to quantity of stem cells.

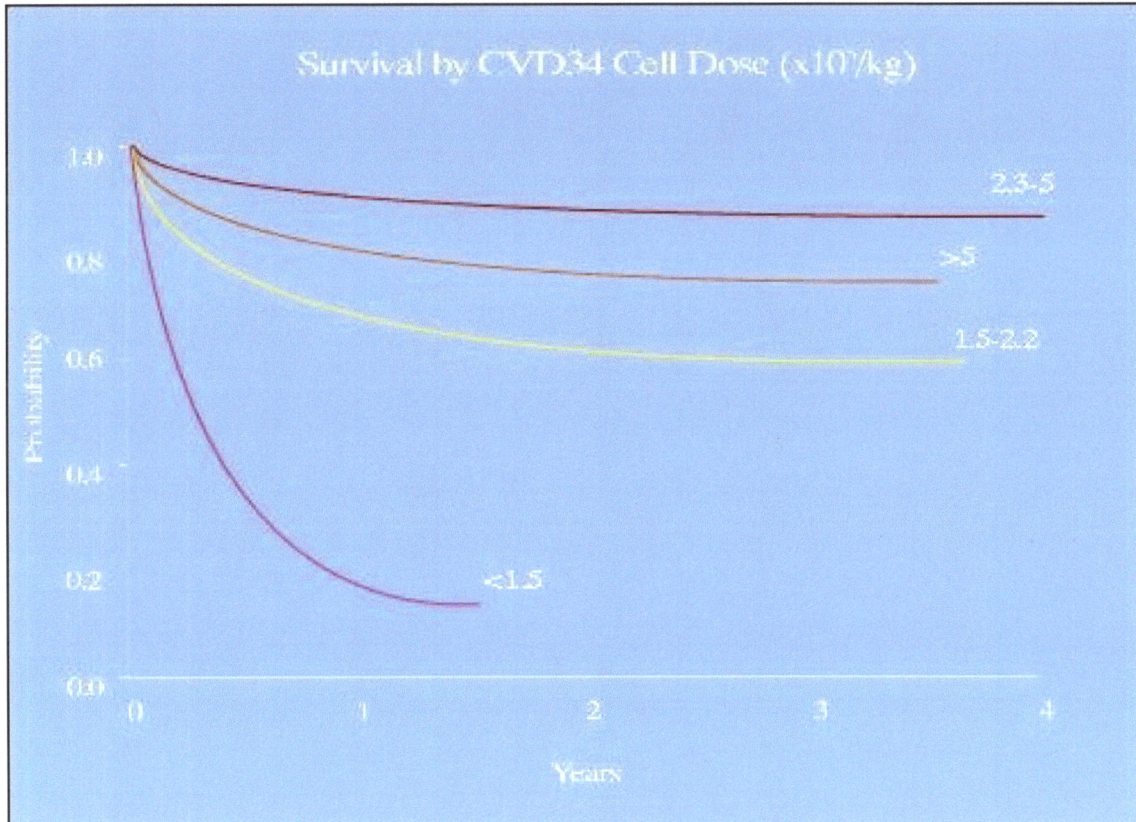

Scientists at the University of Minnesota seek to "expand" umbilical cord blood stem cells, because research has shown that the higher the dose of cells, the faster the transplanted cells will engraft and the better the chance of a cure.

LifeCord, Inc.

Congratulations.
You're going to have a baby!
But what should you be doing to prepare, right now?

Enrolling in Lifecord's Cord Blood Banking Service requires the completion of the following forms:

- ☐ Medical Health History Questionnaire
  This is a simple form to include the parents' health history, as well as the health history of the extended families of the child.

- ☐ Informed Consent for Collection and Storage of the Cord Blood and Maternal Blood
  This form when signed by the expectant mother, signifies that she understands and consents to the procedure for collection of the cord blood by an obstetrician or certified midwife.

- ☐ Informed Consent for the Testing for Infectious Disease
  This form when signed by the expectant mother, signifies that she understands and agrees to the testing of the cord blood and maternal blood through the use of a sample of what was collected during the collection procedure.

- ☐ Liability and Release Form
  This form, when signed by the expectant mother, signifies her agreement that Lifecord's liability will be limited to any amount paid to Lifecord, and releases Lifecord, her obstetrician, Lifecord's obstetrician and the hospital for any liability associated with the collection process.

- ☐ Liability and Release Form
  This form, when signed by the expectant mother, signifies her agreement that Lifecord makes no guarantees in the treatment or process involving the cord blood and maternal blood collected in accordance with this enrollment agreement.

- ☐ Enrollment Agreement
  This agreement is between the mother and Lifecord in which the mother agrees and consents to all the terms and conditions for the performance of the procedure to collect the cord blood and the cryogenic preservation of the cord blood.

- ☐ Checklist
  This checklist should be included in your set of forms, listed above, and checked to ensure that all of these forms have been included.

Enrollment is as simple as any of these:
FAX this form to 1-800-324-3030, 24 hours a day, 7 days a week; or
MAIL these forms to us at 3030 Elgin Lane, Hopesville, California 99890; or
DOWNLOAD these forms from www.lifecord.com and fax or mail completed forms.
If you have any questions, please do not hesitate to call us at 1-800-324-3030, and we will be happy to assist you.

LifeCord, Inc.
Enrollment Agreement

This enrollment agreement between the expectant mother and Lifecord, Inc. provides for the collection and storage of your child=s cord blood from the date of receipt by Lifecord until the child reaches eighteen years of age.

The undersigned mother, _____*Sally Madden*_____ agrees to be the custodian of the cord blood until the child reaches eighteen years of age, and thereafter, the child will take all right and ownership of the cord blood. Upon reaching eighteen years of age, the child must sign an agreement with Lifecord in order to continue to storage of the child=s cord blood.

The enrollment fee for this storage service is $2,000 for enrollees in the United States and Puerto Rico, $2,500 in Canada, and $3,000 for any other country. Multiple births will require an addition payment of $1,000 per each additional child, payable within 4 months of the births. A non-refundable deposit of $100 is required with this enrollment agreement, $1,000 within 10 days after the birth, and the balance within six months after the date of delivery. Annual fee for this service is $250 and will be due on the child=s birthday, beginning with the first birthday.

If at any time you choose to terminate this agreement, you must notify Lifecord in writing. That notification must include whether or not you elect to transfer the cord blood to another cord blood unit facility or whether you choose to transfer all rights to the cord blood to Lifecord.

Lifecord may terminate this agreement upon written notice if for any reason you fail to pay any required fees in accordance with this agreement within forty-five days of any due date. Upon termination of this agreement by Lifecord for non-payment, all rights to the cord blood will be transferred to Lifecord and will terminate any and all contractual obligations between the parties to this agreement.

We further agree that any changes to this agreement must be in writing, and this agreement will be governed by the laws of the state of New Columbia, in the event of a dispute.

I, _____*Sally Madden*_____,
have read and understood this enrollment agreement and I have been given the opportunity to ask any questions I might have about the collection procedure, storage and payment for this service, and they have been answered to my satisfaction. I certify that the information I have given Lifecord is true and correct to the best of my knowledge.

__Sally Madden__	__*Sally Madden*__	__11-20-2010__
Parent1/Mother's full name	Parent 2/Mother's signature	Date
__Jerry Madden__	__*Jerry Madden*__	__Nov. 20, 2010__ .
Parent2/Father's full name	Parent2/Father's signature	Date

Payment must be included and paid by credit card. We agree to the payment of the enrollment fee and to the payment schedule for each additional payment using the following credit card:

☐ Visa   ☐ Mastercard   ☑ American Express   ☐ Discover

____13715 456789 43211____   __12__ / __2018__
Card number   Expiration Date

____Sally Madden____   __11-20-2010__
Signature   Date

LIFECORD, INC.

Informed Consent for Collection and Storage of Cord Blood and Maternal Blood

I understand that my obstetrician or certified midwife will be responsible for the collection of the cord blood at the time of birth, and will make all decisions regarding the life and health of the mother and the child during childbirth. I understand that complications may occur at childbirth, making collection impossible.

Unless the obstetrician/physician or certified midwife determine otherwise, I consent to the following procedures:

1. The collection of cord blood after the birth of my child;

2. The blood typing, nucleated cell, stem cell concentration test, human leukocyte antigen test, infectious disease tests and bacteria and fungus tests performed on my child=s cord blood to determine the quality and condition of the cord blood; and

3. The drawing of my own blood for blood typing and infectious disease testing.

I understand that there are risks associated with the removal of blood which include redness, bruising, discomfort or inflammation around the needle site of the blood withdrawal. Benefits from this withdrawal include the ability to test for blood type and infectious diseases to ensure the safe storage of the cord blood of the child.

I understand that the cord blood may be used in stem cell therapy to treat such diseases as leukemia, certain cancers, and blood disorders. However, I also understand that this therapy may not be effective.

I understand that my child or my family may never withdraw or use the cord blood.

I consent to the inspection of my records by local, state and federal officials as required by law.

I, ___Sally Madden_____, have read and understood this informed consent and confirm that a representative of Lifecord has discussed the contents of this informed consent agreement with me and has answered my questions to my satisfaction. I further agree that I have signed this agreement knowing that I am consenting to this procedure and the contents of this form, and have signed voluntarily.

___Sally Dewhurst Madden___   ___Sally Dewhurst Madden___   ___11-20-2010___
Parent1/Mother's signature   Parent1/Mother's full name   Date

___Jerry Madden___   ___Jerry Dean Madden___   ___Nov. 20, 2010___
Parent2/Father's signature   Parent2/Father's full name   Date

LIFECORD, INC
Medical Health History Questionnaire

Parent1/Mother's Full Name __Sally Madden__   Parent2/Father's full name __Jerry Dean Madden__

Parent1/Mother's Maiden Name __Dewhurst__   Parent2/Mother's Date of Birth __4-5-1960__

Parent1/Mother's Social Security # __520-76-9876__   Home Phone __672-4555__

E-mail address __sally.madden@gmail.com__   Office Phone __675-8732__

Address __1234 54th Avenue__   City __Bellville__   State __N. Col.__   Zip __34590__

Delivery Hospital __Bellville City Hospital__

Hospital Address __1789 Main St.__   City __Bellville__   State __N. Col.__   Zip __34591__

Nurse's Station Phone Number __675-8744__

Expected Due Date _____   Ethnicity _____

OB/CNM Name __Julie Dean, M.D,__   OB/CNM Phone __675-3322__

	Mother		Father	
IN THE PAST YEAR, HAVE YOU OR THE BIOLOGICAL FATHER:	Yes	No	Yes	No
1. Visited or lived in an area endemic for malaria?	( )	(x)	( )	(x)
2. Tested positive or been treated for sexually transmitted diseases?	( )	(x)	( )	(x)
3. Been exposed to hepatitis or jaundice or given gamma globulin?	( )	(x)	( )	(x)
4. Received blood, blood products, derivatives or a tissue or organ transplant?	( )	(x)	( )	(x)
5. Received any vaccinations or Rh immune globulin? ( )	(x)	( )	(x)	
6. Had a tattoo, ear or skin piercing or acupuncture?	(x)	( )	( )	(x)
7. Have you had any prolonged weight loss or weight gain?	( )	(x)	( )	(x)
HEALTH OF MOTHER AND THE BIOLOGICAL FATHER:				
8. Do you have any major health problems or complaints?	( )	(x)	( )	(x)
9. Are you taking any medications?	(x)	( )	( )	( )
10. Have you spent 6 mos or more in Great Britain between 1980-1998?	( )	(x)	( )	( )
11. Have you used any bovine-based insulin which was not US licensed? ( )	(x)	( )	( )	
12. Have you taken any growth hormone under any brand name? ( )	(x)	( )	( )	
13. Have you had any complications with this pregnancy?	( )	(x)	( )	( )
HAS ANYONE IN YOUR IMMEDIATE FAMILY HAD ANY OF THESE?				
14. Aplastic anemia, Fanconi anemia, sickle cell anemia, thalessemia, chronic granulomatosis, Hunter's or Hurler's or any other storage disorder Severe Combined Immunodeficiency Syndrome, Wiskott-Aldrich Syndrome Or any form of leukemia?	(x)	( )	( )	( )
15. Creutzfeldt-Jakob Disease?	( )	(x)	( )	( )
16. Any inherited or genetic disorder?	( )	(x)	( )	( )
17. Do you have more than one relative with any of these diseases?	(x)	( )	( )	( )
HAVE YOU EVER . . . (If yes, please explain)				
18. Had a history of alcohol abuse?	( )	(x)	( )	( )
19. Been diagnosed with a blood or bleeding disorder? ( )	(x)	( )	( )	
20. Been diagnosed with malaria, Chagas' disease or babesiosis? ( )	(x)	( )	( )	
21. Tested positive for Epstein Barr? ( )	(x)	( )	( )	
22. Had hepatitis, yellow jaundice, liver disease or a positive blood test for hepatitis ( )	(x)	( )	( )	
23. Had any infections, surgery or serious illness such as cancer, heart, skin, kidney, lung disease, or diabetes? ( )	(x)	( )	( )	
24. Had hepatitis, yellow jaundice, liver disease, AIDS, HTLV or tested positive?	( )	(x)	( )	( )
25. Had head or brain surgery with a transplant of dura mater?	( )	(x)	( )	( )
26. Donated blood or had a blood transfused to a patient who later showed signs of hepatitis, HIV or HTLV?	( )	(x)	( )	( )
27. Tested positive for AIDS or HIV? ( )	(x)	( )	( )	

PLEASE EXPLAIN ANY "YES" ANSWER AND RECORD THE QUESTION NUMBER:

__17. estranged aunt with leukemia__

I certify that I have answered the above questions truthfully and to the best of my knowledge.

Sally Madden   __11-20-2000__   _Jerry Madden_   _11-20-2000_

Signature of Parent1/Mother   Date   Signature of Parent2/Father   Date

LifeCord, Inc.

Informed Consent for Testing for Infectious Disease and Genetic Predispositions

Lifecord is required by federal law to conduct testing of a sample of cord blood for storage in the facility to determine if there are infectious diseases present in the blood. These diseases include human immunodeficiency virus (HIV), hepatitis B and hepatitis C virus, human lymphotrophic virus, alanine aminotransferase and syphilis. If the blood sample tests positive for any one or more of these diseases, the cord blood may not be accepted for storage by Lifecord.

Lifecord also tests for genetic predispositions to leukemia, certain cancers and blood disorders, where such genetic tests are known and available. This information may be helpful in the determination to continue storage of cord blood for the child.

I understand that the cord blood in conjunction with stem cell therapy may not be an effective treatment for genetic predispositions discovered in Lifecord's testing of cord blood.

I understand that my child or my family may never withdraw or use the cord blood.

I consent to the inspection of my records by local, state and federal officials as required by law.

I, _____Sally Madden_____, have read and understood this information contained in this form and all of my question shave been answered to my satisfaction. I agree to the withdrawal of my child=s blood and cord blood for the tests described in this form. I also agree to the release of these test results to my obstetrician/physician or certified midwife, named below. I further agree that I have signed this agreement knowing that I am consenting to this procedure and the contents of this form, and have signed voluntarily.

Sally Dewhurst Madden	Sally Madden	11-20-2010
Parent1/Mother's full name	Parent1/Mother's signature	Date

Jerry Dean Madden	Jerry Madden	Nov. 20, 2010
Parent2/Father's full name	Parent2/Father's signature	Date

Julie Dean, M.D.	Julie Dean, M.D.	11-20-2010
Obstetrician/physician/midwife	Signature	Date

_____7558903827166_____
Physician/midwife registration number

Jerry and Sally Madden
1234 54th Street
Bellsville, New Columbia

849

46-985
423

Pay to the Order of _Lifecord, Inc._ $ _100.00_

One hundred and no/100———————————————————————————— Dollars

Bellville State Bank

352 Main Street Bellville, NCol 34590   _Jerry Madden—————_

1: 1132554371: 489665"' 849
28988

Loren McCaffery '

FOR DEPOSIT ONLY
LIFECORD, INC.
Acct # 334987622 0
_11-25-00_

Jerry and Sally Madden
1234 54th Street
Bellsville, New Columbia

853

46-985
423

Pay to the Order of ___ Lifecord, Inc. ___ $ 1,000.00

One thousand and no/100————————————————— Dollars

Bellville State Bank

352 Main Street Bellville, NCol 34590   _____ Jerry Madden————

1: 1132554371: 489665"' 853
28988

Loren McCaffery   '

FOR DEPOSIT ONLY
LIFECORD, INC.
Acct # 334987622 0
11-29-00

Jerry and Sally Madden
1234 54th Street
Bellsville, New Columbia

864

December 12, 2010

46-985
423

Pay to the Order of _____ *Lifecord, Inc.* _____ $ *200.00*

Two hundred and no/100————————————————— Dollars

Bellville State Bank

352 Main Street Bellville, N Col 34590

Jerry Madden

1: 1132554371: 489665"' 864

28988

Loren McCaffery '

FOR DEPOSIT ONLY
LIFECORD, INC.
Acct # 334987622 0
12-16-00

Jerry and Sally Madden
1234 54th Street
Bellsville, New Columbia

885

January 12, 2011

46-985
423

Pay to the Order of ___ *Lifecord, Inc.* ___ $ *200.00*

Two hundred and no/100 ———————————————— Dollars

Bellville State Bank

352 Main Street Bellville, NCol 34590

Jerry Madden

1: 1132554371: 489665″′ 885
28988

Loren McCaffery '

FOR DEPOSIT ONLY
LIFECORD, INC.
Acct # 334987622 0
1-16-01

Jerry and Sally Madden
1234 54th Street
Bellsville, New Columbia

899

February 11, 2011

46-985
423

Pay to the Order of _____ Lifecord, Inc. _____ $ 200.00

Two hundred and no/100———————————————————— Dollars

Bellville State Bank

352 Main Street Bellville, N Col 34590

Jerry Madden

1: 1132554371: 489665"' 899
28988

Loren McCaffery

FOR DEPOSIT ONLY
LIFECORD, INC.
Acct # 334987622 0
2-14-01

Jerry and Sally Madden
1234 54th Street
Bellsville, New Columbia

919

March 10, 2011

46-985
423

Pay to the Order of _____ *Lifecord, Inc.* _____ $ *200.00*

Two hundred and no/100 ———————————————— Dollars

Bellville State Bank

352 Main Street Bellville, N Col 34590

Jerry Madden

1: 1132554371: 489665"' 919
28988

Loren McCaffery

FOR DEPOSIT ONLY
LIFECORD, INC.
Acct # 334987622 0
3-16-01

Jerry and Sally Madden
1234 54th Street
Bellsville, New Columbia

936

April 11, 2011

46-985
423

Pay to the Order of _____ Lifecord, Inc. _____ $ 200.00

Two hundred and no/100 _____ Dollars

Bellville State Bank

352 Main Street Bellville, N Col 34590

Jerry Madden

1: 1132554371: 489665"' 936
28988

Loren McCaffery

FOR DEPOSIT ONLY
LIFECORD, INC.
Acct # 334987622 0
4-14-01

Jerry and Sally Madden
1234 54th Street
Bellsville, New Columbia

955

May 12, 2011

46-985
423

Pay to the Order of ___ Lifecord, Inc. ___ $ 200.00

Two hundred and no/100————————————— Dollars

Bellville State Bank

352 Main Street Bellville, N Col 34590

Jerry Madden

1: 1132554371: 489665"' 955
28988

Loren McCaffery

FOR DEPOSIT ONLY
LIFECORD, INC.
Acct # 334987622 0
5-13-01

Jerry and Sally Madden
1234 54th Street
Bellsville, New Columbia

1122

June 11, 2011

46-985
423

Pay to the Order of _____ Lifecord, Inc. _____ $ 200.00

Two hundred and no/100————————————————— Dollars

Bellville State Bank

352 Main Street Bellville, N Col 34590

Jerry Madden

1: 1132554371: 489665"' 1122
28988

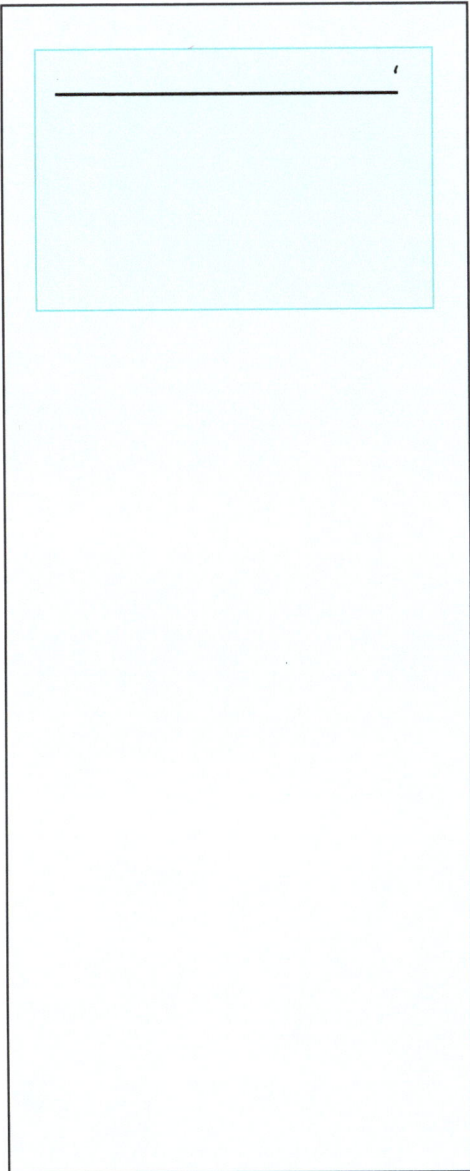

Account Name _____ Mr. and Mrs. Jerry Madden _____

Account number _____ 435–2000 _____

Date Due	Date Received	Payment Amount	Form of Payment
Nov 20	Nov 25	$ 100·00	check #849
Nov 30	Nov 29	$ 1,000·00	check #853
Dec 15	Dec 16	$ 200·00	check #864
Jan 15	Jan 16	$ 200·00	check #885
Feb 15	Feb 14	$ 200·00	check # 899
Mar 15	Mar 16	$ 200·00	check #919
Apr 15	Apr 14	$ 200·00	check # 936
May 15	May 13	$ 200·00	check #955
June 15	Not received		

Time	Caller	Reason/Referred to	Subject
8:00a	Biogene	sales pool	sales
8:15	Sam Good	Jan Weston	inspection
8:20	Oncolever		sales
8:29	Donna LaFalce	Susie Boren	sales
9:15	Genex	Jan Weston	sales
10:35	Generation IX	Susie Boren	sales
10:36	Forrest Childs	pool	?
11:04	Jerry Downing		info
11:15	Sarah Whitting	Dr. Sorenson	info
11:28	Donna LaFalce	Susie Boren	sales
11:35	(hang up)		———
11:46	Jacob Levinson	Jan Weston	info
11:55	Donna LaFalce	Susie Boren	info
12:00n	Kimberly Wade		info
12:10p	Jim Sandoval		sales
12:19	Jessica Steward	Jan Weston	info
12:40	Jimmy Doral		info
1:10	Fawn Hendrix	Dr. Sorenson	info
1:15	Sally Jennings	Susie Boren	info
1:22	June Riley	Jan Weston	info
1:34	Kim Finnegan	pool	sales
1:55	Cary Lenard	pool	sales
2:04	Pam Sinclair	pool	info

XII. Applicable Statutes

The applicable statutes as follows for the state of New Columbia are the choice of law for this litigation in the federal district court. The Federal Rules of Evidence are the applicable rules of evidence.

Applicable Statutes

Negligence

32 N. Col. § 298
Negligence.

When an act is negligent only if done without reasonable care, the care which the actor has a duty to exercise to avoid being negligent in the doing of the act is that which a reasonable man in his position, with his information and competence, or is the industry standard, would recognize as necessary to prevent the act from creating an unreasonable risk of harm to another.

Products Liability Act

32 N.Col. § 2.
Liability of Seller or Distributor for Harm Caused by Defective Products

One engaged in the business of selling or otherwise distributing products who sells or distributes a defective product is subject to liability for harm to persons or property caused by the defect.

§ 1. *Definitions.*
Defective product. A product is defective when, at the time of sale or distribution, it contains a manufacturing defect, is defective in design, or is defective because of inadequate instructions or warnings. A product:

(a) contains a manufacturing defect when the product departs from its intended design even though all possible care was exercised in the preparation and marketing of the product; or

(b) is defective in design when the foreseeable risks of harm posed by the product could have been reduced or avoided by the adoption of a reasonable alternative design by the seller or other distributor, or a predecessor in the commercial chain of distribution, and the omission of the alternative design renders the product not reasonably safe.

Medical Malpractice

2 N. Col. § 6.02
Sec. 6.02. In a suit against a physician or health care provider involving a health care liability claim that is based on the failure of the physician or health care provider to disclose or adequately to disclose the risks and hazards involved in the medical care or surgical procedure rendered by the physician or health care provider, the only theory on which recovery may be obtained is that of negligence in failing to disclose the risks or hazards that could have influenced a reasonable person in making a decision to give or withhold consent.

Wrongful Death

32 N. Col. § 667
Wrongful death statute provides:
Whenever the death of a person is caused by wrongful act, neglect, or default such as would have entitled the party injured to maintain an action to recover damages if death had not ensued, the person who would have been liable if death had not ensued is liable to an action for damages, even though the death was caused under circumstances as amount in law to murder in the first or second degree, or manslaughter. If the person so liable dies, the action may be brought against the executor or administrator of his estate. If he left no estate within the State of New Columbia, the court may appoint an administrator upon application.

Conversion

32 N. Col. § 222
Liability for Dispossession

One who dispossesses another of a chattel is subject to liability in trespass for the damage done. If the dispossession seriously interferes with the right of the other to control the chattel, the actor may also be subject to liability for conversion.

Breach of Contract

14 N. Col. § 231
Criterion for Determining When Performances Are to Be Exchanged Under an Exchange of Promises

Performances are to be exchanged under an exchange of promises if each promise is at least part of the consideration for the other and the performance of each promise is to be exchanged at least in part for the performance of the other.

14 N. Col. § 346

Availability of Damages (1) The injured party has a right to damages for any breach by a party against whom the contract is enforceable unless the claim for damages has been suspended or discharged. (2) If the breach caused no loss or if the amount of the loss is not proved under the rules stated in this Chapter, a small sum fixed without regard to the amount of loss will be awarded as nominal damages.

Misrepresentation

32 N. Col. § 9

Liability of Commercial Product Seller or Distributor for Harm Caused by Misrepresentation

One engaged in the business of selling or otherwise distributing products who, in connection with the sale of a product, makes a fraudulent, negligent, or innocent misrepresentation of material fact concerning the product is subject to liability for harm to persons or property caused by the misrepresentation.

32 N. Col. §159
Misrepresentation Defined

A misrepresentation is an assertion that is not in accord with the facts.

www.ingramcontent.com/pod-product-compliance
Lightning Source LLC
Chambersburg PA
CBHW041446210326
41599CB00004B/146